The Penguin Club

By Chet Shedleski

Inspired by Tom Barton

Copyright 2014 All Rights Reserved

Published by The Book Shed

ISBN 978-0-9906061-3-0

I

I don't want to die but right now I wouldn't mind. Riding a beach cruiser with a tire that barely holds air for the duration of a thirty block trek from center city Philly makes ya forget the lighter parts of life. It's sleeting. Can't keep my eyes open for more than a few seconds at a time without real pain. I ride with my eyes closed through lights of green or red - hundred bucks after working fourteen hours at the bar makes for some indifference to most things. This could have been avoided, but I'm much smarter than my dad. Now he can say 'I told you so'. He won't. He doesn't have to.

I think I forgot to do it for this go around. It doesn't really matter either way. Both end up in tears and me being an asshole. It's just easier to defend myself against the unknowing public when I can cite examples of me telling the truth about everything from the beginning. Although that only goes so far as well. "You're still an asshole!" I'll hear. I don't believe it, but when you hear something so often...

"What are we doing?"
"Going to the mall to get me a shirt so I don't look like a slob"

I know what she is asking but a joke always loosens up the conversation and allows for serious comments to be taken as a joke which always works in my favor.

"Shut up! You know what I mean!"
"Yeah I know. I was just kiddin' around. Well... except the slob part..."
"Stop it."
"Sorry... Ummm hangin' out and such? Why?
"Just hanging out?"
"You obviously want a certain answer what is it?"

It is always interesting seeing where these conversations end up taking place. The build up is usually begun with an awkward, detached greeting followed by small talk that of strangers while going somewhere at least fifteen minutes away. Instead of talking about anything serious in this time, comments about another shitty, overcast day flood the air. This works in my favor, providing time for me to build my generic, non-threatening, vague answers to pretty much anything anyone could possibly come up with. This one ends up in the mall parking lot still in the car. The car is turned off and she stares at me like I just asked her to get an abortion. This doesn't make sense since she isn't pregnant.

"Am I wasting my time with you?"
"Probably. Why?" knowing that this would piss her off a bit.
"Be serious for once."

"Well I'm not hanging out with anyone else like us if that's what you're wondering."
"Well I didn't think so but thanks for telling me." most likely worried about this.
"Honestly I don't know what this is. I just am kinda goin' with it."
"Well I guess that's good."

I could have said anything not involving fucking someone else and she would have said the same thing, maybe a little more excitedly if I were drunk and a little more generous, but you get the point. Vague answers cover all. You would think I feel bad, but so many girls have done it to me. Where do you think I know this stuff from? I don't read, that's for sure. Karma is a bitch I guess.

This interaction subdues her for now. We go into the mall. We go into a trendy store. She picks out a shirt. I don't like it. Ninety dollars later I'm dressing fashionable for a night. She's a girl. She knows what she's doing. I'm a guy. I'm fucked.

I know I come across as an absolute gentlemen, but we've been bonin' for quite a while now. How do you think all this nonsense started? It's good, obviously. Things like this don't last without good ugly bumping. The ugly truth about it though is that the sex drives unwarranted feelings, even for me. We get intimate and the hormones start rushing through me after a little. The next thing you know I'm thinking about her when she's not around. This lasts all of a brief moment, then the next thing I know I'm scheming up ways of getting her out of bed so I can sprawl across my small floored mattress.

Usually when my feelings become a factor in my daily actions I take certain precautionary measures to avoid tricking myself into liking whoever the girl is at the time. First thing to do when I can't get her out of my mind is to jerk the hell off. For a majority of the time if I do this I can't even remember what the girl looks like, her name or that I'm supposed to call her at some point. I then realize that it is all just a physical attraction. It's easier to navigate the pseudo relationship with the compass between my legs de-magnetized for a little bit. Then I can tell the girl that nothing is ever going to come from whatever it is that's going on. Coupled with that, I inform her that if she does start developing feelings over and above sweating all over each other, she has to tell me. Typically she'll laugh at this thinking to herself "I could never have feelings for this asshole." I'll insist and she'll insist back with another laugh. I laugh, of course because she is wrong. However, if the fun way of figuring out that I don't like someone fails, there's another step - picture her plus 300 hundred pounds. I'm attracted to physically fit girls. It would be hard for me to continue being with someone if they somehow gained 300 pounds. It sounds bad, but shut the hell up. This one usually works. Rarely do I have to do anything else besides this. But, if somehow that doesn't bother me or I'm in some sort of phase of my life that condones that sorta taste, I simply picture her shitting. Picture a real shit, no little rabbit turds, but rather the runny-assed shit that you're almost embarrassed to let go around your friends that leaves you screaming with shit somehow on top of the toilet seat by some shit miracle. If I can stand the idea of something as smelly and disgusting as I let go out of my ass earlier coming out of her, then there may be some grounds for the weird feelings I'm having.

If I get through all these, then I'm really fucked.

II

Tonight there is a party, a party thrown by our two married friends, a party for couples. We are a couple. We are going. It's one of those events that she planned for us without any input from me. I don't really care much but this is a huge pet peeve of mine. I hate having my plans planned out for me without my consent. I consent to everything so just tell me. I like these people, but not my uninvolvement with the plans, damn it!

Tonight comes quickly against my unconscious will. I'm wearing the shirt we got me today. At a second glance it looks pretty great. I'm really excited about the shirt now, anything to keep my mind off the fact that I wasn't involved in the planning process on coming here, even though I would not have cared anyway.

We drive up to their house. It's your standard first home for newly weds. There is a lot of attention to stupid details, most likely to make up for the fact that it's not their dream house. Maybe it's just what normal people do with their houses. I don't really care. We park on the street. With a deep sigh I open the door and step out. We walk up the side walk. This is where we probably should be holding hands or something, nope... With another deep sigh I ring the doorbell and wait.

"What's wrong with you?"
"Nothing. Why?"
"You seem pissed."
"Do I?" semi-sarcastic and uninterested
"Yes."
"Well.. Sorry"

Door opens right on cue with my happy face. We are greeted with a jubilant shriek and a bottle of wine. Hugs and kisses are thrown around everywhere to everyone. We are neither early or late so most are here. Like a shot of a gun I head for one, maybe a beer as well, possibly a wine night, too.

I find myself in the kitchen with a girl I don't know, must be from an outsider couple. We introduce and make small talk. Like any decent human, she is nice and polite. Like any self-loathing ass, I'm dismissively sarcastic with my remarks. The sarcasm is lost but the humor is not, not sure how, but it isn't. Shots?

Seeing that I'm not too uptight, she lets her guard down from our initial greeting, nothing too absurd, but down either way. She talks about how she's uncomfortable tonight because she doesn't know anyone. I say I'm uncomfortable because I know everyone. I'm not sure what this means but neither does she. She laughs. Shots?

This mindless banter goes on for however long with a few more shots mixed throughout. After the last one I realize that I'm feeling it a bit. She must be smashed. I have a tendency to get people drunk without realizing it. She will be a little looser at least. Hopefully she can handle herself. Hopefully I can handle myself. I remember that I'm here with someone. It dawns on me that I've been acting like a child and I don't even know why, like a bad pouting child.

Besides the occasional drunk friend wandering in for a drink with a coinciding hello, I've been pretty anti-social. I'm probably, most likely, definitely in some sort of trouble with the lady. Well, one more shot for the hallway. Jesus I'm a miserable person, a shot to that as well.

I walk into the living room. It's a decent sized living room. They have pictures of how happy they are together, living plants and matching furniture. It scares me to see this, only because I know they are just that much closer to the married couple realm where they only hang out with couples. Of course, who am I to talk? I'm here as half a couple. That's actually the scary part. Hang around them enough and the topics-of-conversation river runs dry leaving a desperate pack of coupled nomads; occasionally quenching our thirst with thoughts of marriage or kids. Babies. Me? I Never thought I'd be so pro-not-pulling-out. Regardless, I don't see me trying to have a baby on purpose any time soon. Especially with what's-her-face.

She is fun though

I see her at the end of the L-ed couch. I'm in the drunk for some mature female companionship. I ignore her blatant signs of disgust, hop over the coffee table like it's my place and sit down. She's obviously pissed at me. I'm obviously teetering on piss drunk. She knows it too - results of hanging around her for so long. There's one course of action in these instances of such lopsided inebriation: be really silly, not drunk mess stupid, but silly, flirty, couple stupid.

"What's up?" I say in a way a puppy would if its ancestors mated with apes instead of other dogs - we've all been there.
"Where have you been?" she says in a way a pissed off girlfriend would sound when her shit-faced, half dog, half monkey boyfriend plopped down beside her.
"I've been in the kitchen talking with that girl from the couple we don't know"
"You spent how long in there and you don't even know her name? Wait, you're probably too drunk to remember."

Wow. Succinct. No point in arguing this one. It's not the time to have an ego about whether or not I'm drunk, especially since I am - noting that I have a stupid little smile on my face from just now noticing the small spot of cleavage from her shirt that almost but doesn't fit correctly. Anything I say right now she will dismiss without thought. Like I said, we've been hanging around each other long enough for her to know when I'm getting a little rambunctious. People are affected by booze differently: sad, mad, happy, flirty, loud, abusive, mean, quiet, gay. There are definite reasons some girls like some of these things. You know, the mean and abusive thing, I do not understand, but apparently there's psychology stuff that explains it like common sense. The happy, flirty drunk I can understand. What girl doesn't like a guy that smiles around her and publicly flirts in front of other people? Weird ones, but that's not the point here. Even better, what girl doesn't like an outwardly apologetic boyfriend that admits when he's wrong and at least pretends to do something about it. Yeah I'm a jello shooter away from the spins and some deep tantric breathing with one of the toilets in the house, but I'm sure something will work out in my favor.

"You know what babe? I did take some shots in there and I'm a little tipsy (hammered). I never thought to ask her name. I guess I figured I'd figure it out later through group conversation. I'm sorry I've been a whiny bitch all night. You don't deserve it and I'm not even sure why I was acting like that. You think we can sneak out to the car and get all naked?"

She is taken off by the honesty and probably slightly turned on by the car idea.

"You're an ass"
"Oh is that so?" squeezing her knee for a quick jerk and a high pitch laugh.
"Stop it" in a loud whisper with a mean happy face.

Might as well be a moan and a blatant prophylactic falling out of her bag.

I like this.

I can see myself with her.

This is usually the point where I try and stop myself. The mix of booze and the company of a girl that doesn't annoy me tends to trend towards serious feelings, like love or some shit close to it. I've said many times before, I do not want be tricked into loving someone, especially by myself. It's happened a few times before, none ending in any sort of positive. I can't tell if I'm pulling a fast one on myself (emotionally not physically because that's usually pretty obvious) or if I'm actually getting something here. It sounds stupid, especially since this has come out of a stupid mini argument that I've dealt with many times before, but this time seems a little different, not too much, but different either way. Jesus hell, it's happening again. Just thinking about it is a confession to guilt. I don't think it matters. I'll be in drunken auto-pilot mode soon anyway.

The night continues like most things do despite my best efforts. Board games are broken out. Bottles of wine clutter the counter tops. My nameless shot buddy has to go. Her boyfriend found her passed out on the toilet - nothing gross like vomiting, just shitting uncontrollably. The dude carries her out the front reciting a string of apologies and possible explanations as to how this could've happened.

"She never gets like this. She must be sick"

I laugh and tug down the shirt with the small cleavage spot while they're all watching.

Everyone wonders how she got so drunk.

The night continues even more. I feel like it's been a while more than it probably has been. One couple asks to grab a spare room, they had three bottles between them. Another drives home against the general consensus. They are adults. They can make decisions, immature ones, but decisions at the least. God only knows what the other couples do. The lady of the house announces herself drunk while already half way upstairs. "Shankss fur commmmminnnnggg!!!" The stragglers consist of me, the man of the house and my passed out girl - head resting on my thigh with an afghan covering half her torso.

"You got a keeper there don't ya?" nodding at her.
"Seems like it"
"Lucky bastard"

Sounds promising.

He wanders upstairs to find his princess most likely passed out fully clothed with her face hanging off the foot of the bed.

She's on my lap passed out. I can probably drive, but getting a drunk sleeping girl home right now would totally kill my buzz. Surprisingly, what does appeal to me is the thought *at least I can spend the night with her,* like the past hundred nights spent together were lost and forgotten.

I find a pillow within reach and finagle it around to fit under head. By some guy magic I manage to do this while bringing her up to my end of the couch to join me. She doesn't wake up. Although, I wouldn't mind if she did. She's probably just ignoring me, but at least she is here with me. I lay there with her nestled in my shoulder. The curse/blessing of being able to hold my booze haunts me for some time. Not drunk enough to pass out, too drunk to stop thinking about everything in a way that makes me think too much. This girl is great. What the hell am I waiting for? Something better probably. Let's stop kidding myself, I'm not finding anything better. I think I love this girl. I love this girl. I don't, but it seems the right time and place to think so. Every thought going through my head leads to something else and then on to another something or other. I'm with a girl that likes me more than reasonably so, asleep on my lap. I'm a huge prick.

"Why am I thinking like this?"
"It's probably just because you're fucked up right now."
"Why would all this shit come up now?"
"Probably because you are alone in a room with a tolerable girl on your lap."
"Yep. That's probably it."
"You should get out before it sucks a lot."
"But maybe I really do like her, maybe even love her."
"Well let's go through the reasons why you're being an idiot right now... You got smashed immediately. There were a bunch of other couples there so naturally your childish tendencies surfaced and you wanted something you don't have."
"But I do have that"
"Shut up... She fell for your stupid bullshit and didn't get mad even though you were inappropriately drunk."
"I wasn't drunk"
"..."
"What?"
"Lastly, you've been talking to yourself since the dude left. Go to bed. It'll wear off in the morning..."

I dream of something absurd and unrelated to anything that is going on. I think it involves some dinosaurs, a falling sequence and my great grandfather who died on my fourth birthday who's usually suffocating me with a vacuum in another reoccurring dream of mine. I realize I'm dreaming at some point and decide to fly. It's always towards someone. I fly to the dinosaur and ask how my great grandfather can be here... he's dead. The monster looks at me and says 'the past is always before the future' The dinosaur isn't attractive so I try to turn him into an attractive blond. Whenever this happens the only girl I can think of is this mildly not ugly girl I knew from grade school, Tricia. Tricia pops out from behind the dinosaur. I'm immediately disappointed with my lack of imagination.

III

I wake up in a cold sweat. My cold sweats are worse than my normal run-a-couple-miles sweats. I wake up completely drenched with nothing to show for it. My metabolism is a phenomenal piece of shit. I wipe my forehead of all the beads. I'm wide awake at this point. I hear the asshole birds chirping. The ones that make you run to bed and bury your head in a pillow because you realize you have to wake up at seven and they're signaling the sun to come up. I haven't heard those birds since my aderol-induced-all-nighters in college. I hate those birds. They never change. It's anywhere from 5:48 to 6:13 judging by those stupid shit birds.

Sober as I was before, maybe even more so, I jostle her for a semi-conscious response.

"What?"
"Let's go home"

With a drunken nod or a passed out head bob she agrees with me. Keys,wallet, phone and her shit. We are ready to go. It's still not light outside but by no means is it dark. I trap her in the car on the passenger and I muddle over to my side while convincing myself I'm not drunk. I spark the engine with a sense of *what the fuck* and set off to a horizon not quite lit with hope, but a promise of a feeling of tomorrow. It's inevitable, unavoidable and unforgivable.

We get back to one of our places, interchangeable at this point. I wake her up from her convenient sleep.

"What?!"
"We are home"

She instantly, as if rehearsed, passes right back to the better side of life. The downer that I am pulls her right back to my reality - getting her inside the house. I drove so she has to walk. She manages to get inside and even to bed, clothed with her head at the foot of the bed. The stupid birds have stopped bitching. The sun is all the way up. Well, not really because it's not noon. My night/morning has come to an end. I have no idea what day it is. I really don't know what's going on. I know I'm home. I know I'm with her. I know tomorrow is going to suck, but at least I will wake up to her.

"You are a stupid, stupid asshole."
"I know"

Some time later I wake up with a mouth full of hair. God only knows where I am right now. He reminds me. Oh yeah. I can't fall back asleep. I roll into different uncomfortable positions until every part of my body hurts - shoulders, elbows, hips, feet some how. I finally find a perfect ratio of shit shoved between my legs and the angle of my arm under my head. Now I have to piss. Contemplating holding it I remember that I pissed her bed last week. She never woke up so I just put my shirt on top of it and fell back asleep. Even if she did wake up I would've blamed it on her.

I get up and piss.

Now fully awake, too fragile to do anything, I lay in bed staring at the ceiling thinking of acceptance speeches for things I haven't done yet and probably never will. I think of better times with a better person. It doesn't really do it for me. If it were that much better I would be there now.

By chance she wakes up, by chance I mean I rumbled around enough making it impossible for her to sleep anymore. Her tired eyes find mine wired.

"Hey."
"Hey."

Here's when someone pours detergent on the shit slide and I go head first out of control into whatever could be worse than a trip down a shit slide. There's none such a helpless, innocent, pure trusting look than when she first wakes up. It gets me. It's like she knows all the bullshit that goes through my head but accepts and actually wants me anyway. There might be a little hope that I can change, but it doesn't really matter. She's taking me 'as is' and hoping for the best.

The euphoric sense of waking engulfs her. The euphoric sense of 'I've been dealing with shit for too long' engulfs me. Our stupid, drunk, tired eyes catch each other. Our stupid, drunk, tired lips meet. Our stupid, drunk, tired selves start doing stupid, tired, drunk things.

I brush the hair from her eyes. She heavily blinks for some reason. I smile like a cocky son-of-a-bitch. She smiles like she likes me for smiling like such. For a time we pretend like nothing matters. For a time we just hump the living shit out of each other. For a time it couldn't be better. For a time it couldn't be worse.

I wake up, look around and declare myself a mess. I see her next to me. At least I know her, pretty well actually. I check the time. It's 11:30 something AM. Shit, at least it's the morning. I nestle her in the shoulder. She doesn't wake up. I gently shake her violently while whispering 'wake the fuck up' in her ear.

'Hey' is what I get with a glimmer and some eye crust. Nicest eye crust I've seen in a while. She knows it's time to go. So we go. No need for good byes, not in my mind.

A month or so passes. Everything seems great. I think I'm starting to climb over my wall of 'just going with it until it gets somewhere, then bailing'. I seem to like her. I even start referring to her as my girlfriend. My friends think there is something wrong with me. I don't get black out drunk every chance I get. I stay in on some weekend nights. I don't wear sweat pants as much. I know there's something wrong with me. I kinda like it.

We do couple things often; dinner, lunch - lots of eating related things - even breakfast since my head's rarely viced in the morning anymore. We talk about stuff other than when we are going to meet next. We text before midnight and even during the day. I ask about parts of her day she doesn't remember telling me about. She comes up in most of my conversations with people who don't know her. She comes over almost every night. We don't have sex every night. I even call her my girlfriend.

During this time I'm happy, at least I've convinced everyone, most importantly myself. I don't think there is much convincing being done. I've been so shut off for so long that I forgot what it's like to like someone. It's slowly coming back.

Give a person a chance and you'll remember how unique we all are. There are no two people exactly alike - similarities yes, but completely unique regardless. For any one person to show any interest in any particular other is just insane. Why? How? Stop thinking of people as one group of billions, but rather a billion independents. Two random individuals come together, matching like nothing else ever in existence before and never will. You can argue location, background, conscious thought but all of that depended on people that came before. Think of the numbers, the chances of that one moment occurring. Makes winning the lottery a flip of a coin. If you're unlucky enough to be able to, think of your children. From the billions of others out there you chose the kid's mother or father. Get real crazy with it and think of the millions of man seeds that could have won the race. Just think, if you did it doggy style instead of splitting wood maybe you have a cancer-curing daughter or a peace-saving son rather than the bar-working shit that wakes up in the afternoon explaining that he works hard and makes good money and that's why he isn't using his 200,000 dollar degree to do anything.

Or maybe we just fuckin'.

"Are you cheating on me?" I ask with a serious smile.
"What?! No! Why would you think that?"
"I dunno..."

"Well there has to be a reason"
"Well..."
"Well what? You can tell me."
"Well... It's just that..." I sigh deeply, almost cough and then kinda laugh because that happened.
"Just that what? What are you laughing at?" in the beginning tones of anger.
"Things are too good right now. So you're either cheating on me, or I'm dreaming."

She hides a smile with the turn of her head and punches me in the chest.

"Ow" lying with a smile.
"You're too cute..."

I hide a smile with a joke that I don't listen to. It's neat I can produce responses without thought. I honestly have no idea what I just said. She's laughing so it doesn't matter. Actually, the funny part of this is that I was completely serious when I asked her if she was cheating on me. I wasn't trying to be cute. I was genuinely concerned. Too many times I've found myself holding hands with a girl I love only to realize my dead grandmother and reoccurring dream dinosaur are playing four square in my grade school parking lot.

"...and funny!"
"If you only knew."
"Knew what?"
"I don't know."

She punches me again. I laugh like it doesn't hurt. She laughs like it does. It may hurt - could go either way.

Another month of social milling about passes, not sure where we are headed, always looking for something better but at the same time realizing it could be worse. Haven't seen anything anyway - haven't been paying much attention. Think I may be liking her like she deserves. No one would guess how much a sleeping beauty keeps me up. I feel guilty like I should be doing something to deserve this.

Time for the day. I let her sleep and head down stairs. It seems anyway that when I disturb things I do exactly that, disturb them. Downstairs I start with my coffee. I'm pretty sure the scoop in the coffee tin isn't the right size. I'm pretty sure I don't care as long as there's at least way more coffee than needed. I scoop four times for two. The mugs are oversized and match. Having nothing to do in the eternity of time it takes to watch a pot brew, I put on some tunes - something funky, hard and soothing. Life is not so terrible at the moment - hasn't been for the last many. Might even say it hasn't been bad.

In mid song I stop and turn. I see her slowly having her way with gravity and the stairs. With her hair a mess and all over the place she wears my undershirt and maybe a set of my boxers I've had since 7th grade. I can't tell - the shirt covers them and I recently bought a couple packs.

"Don't look at me I'm gross"

I don't listen. She's not.

"Oh please... I could punch you in the nose, have you gushing blood and crying and you would still look good."

She's unimpressed. Weird. She usually humors my humor in the morning. Something is stupid in my kitchen.

"Everything ok?"
"Yep."

Ah hah! First clue to an unexpected passive-aggressive scavenger hunt. I'm already uninterested. I hate scavenger hunts so I let it be. We mill about. I avoid eye contact with her as she mopes around the room like I raped her last night.

"Excuse me." I move "Thanks."
"Uhuh"
"Can you pass me a spoon?"
"Yep" passing her a spoon while finding interest in the floor.

This shit keeps going for a bit. I rustle some stuff in a cabinet. She messes with the mess drawer. I walk in circles. She prefers squares. I automatically think she cheated on me. I don't know what she's thinking. That's not uncommon. We are sitting across from each other at the table. She has a bowl of cereal that she finds as fascinating as I did the floor during the spoon pass of five minutes ago. I sit slouching with my legs spread as far as comfortably possible, eyes wandering the kitchen while preparing myself to hear that she's cheating on me. Her cereal must've said something mean because she's starting to cry. Without compromising my high school dropout posture I tilt my head down to the right and just stare at her.

"What's wrong?" running through every possible guy she could've hooked up with in my head.

"I'm pregnant..."

My head goes blank and my body starts to tingle. So this is what it feels like. Haven't felt like this since the last time I smoked pot after a night of getting black out drunk. The feeling and thought is always immediate and the same - I'm going to shit from every hole in my body. Unsure of whether or not I voided my bowels, I pretend to scratch my ass and check if I shit myself. Everything feels tingly so I can't really tell. It doesn't seem like so but I smell my hand just to make sure. My sense of smell is awful so I resort to my 20/20 vision. By this time I forget what I'm doing and run to the bathroom to throw up.

I would give anything right now to be throwing up from an unnecessary 4AM high than what's about to sink in forever.

It hits me like a sack of fat babies, one being mine. Not that I would throw my baby, or any baby, in a sac, but right now I'm thinking a little crooked. I get that sinking heart feeling and I'm forced to clench my butt cheeks in fear of defecating myself for the first time in months. Luckily it has sunk into every other part of my body as well, delaying what I've become disgustingly too familiar with.

I think of all those times I waited that extra second or seven to please her just a little more. Maybe it was for both our benefit. It was all for me. I actually convinced myself long ago that she doesn't get any pleasure out of my mediocrity-ridden-sex-giving at all. She's just nice and lets me hump her like a dog. This all could've been avoided if I didn't hang in there so long. It wasn't worth it. Well, it was then, definitely not now though. To think I had control was so stupid. I don't have control over anything. What made me think I could control this is a mystery.

No mystery.

Just sex.

What about all the people I know that this should be happening to instead of me. There are so many others that deserve this - the ones that brag about pulling out and always ask "what the fuck are condoms?!". What about the guys that have banged more girls than I've said hi to? How have they avoided this? I don't deserve this. I treat babies nice. Maybe that's a detriment in this situation. I hold doors for old people. I yield at yield signs. I don't kill anyone that won't be missed. I pay rent almost on time almost every month. I pull out!

I look around for my dead grandma and her dinosaur friend. Nothing. They're never there when I need them. Son of a bitch. How 'bout that not-so-attractive-yet-not-really-ugly girl from grade school. I've never wanted to see such a mediocre looking girl before. This isn't happening.

This can't be happening.

This is happening.

This is happening.

Christ.

"... and I'm..."

Oh shit she's still talking. On the same sentence too. Well this will be a life test for the ages judged on the reaction to this oncoming intention. I'm a lifelong unpracticing Catholic. I grew up taught that abortion is murder and one of the worst acts a human can do besides gay butt sex. Naive and unquestioning I never thought a second thought about this fact. It's a baby and you can't kill it. Not a difficult choice for a child that has yet to find out how shitty condoms feel.

> *I don't understand how people can kill babies like that...*
>
> *Don't take your irresponsibility out on the unborn kid who had no choice in your late night romp.*
>
> *If you don't want a baby just don't have sex!*

Then puberty came about.

Later the whole choice thing was presented to me. Indifferent and exempt from the situation I understood where women were coming from. It should be there choice to do whatever they want with their body. I do whatever I want with mine, but now I have a girlfriend with my child growing inside. Maybe someone else should have regulated what I was doing. Then I wouldn't be in such a vexing situation.

Instead of thinking of friends that should be getting girls pregnant, I would be doing something constructive. Maybe something like pottery. It would be hard to do anything though considering I would probably be blind. I knew I should have pushed anal a little bit harder.

What do I do? If she wants to keep it... Then it's kept. Even though choice is good and all that, I can't justify pushing the abo-bo. Even suggesting I feel would punch my couch-class ticket to hell. Sinning is bad, but making others sin is apparently a million times worse. There may be a 2% active participation rate among Catholics, but I'll give the guilt a healthy 90% level of effectiveness. I haven't been to church since my high school forced us to and I never really paid attention. The whole time I would be picking out the girls who preferred sitting like boys across the way from me.

The thought of leading her that way ping pongs back and forth in my head. It would have to be indirectly if anything at all.

'Having babies sucks'
'Babies are stupid'
'Have an abortion'

This will not work. I have no ability to hide my emotions, intentions, thoughts, desires or even my pathetic erections. No way I can pull this off, especially with a clean conscience. No one would know, except of course me which would undoubtedly be much worse. Dealing with my feelings has never been tough for me, but I've never had any tough ones to deal with.

What if she doesn't want to keep it? That opens a whole other gateway to mind fuck central station. Let's be serious, no one wants babies besides the dumb and the willing - not necessarily both. The dumb argument for me would be an honest one. I don't want a kid though. So I'm not dumb, just stupid.

If she wants to get rid of it I can't just sit back, smile, say 'Okie doke' and throw a party - would definitely throw party. It's my duty to the church I've been loosely affiliated with my entire life to shepherd the lost sheep to the lost-youth hills of babyville. So I must give a legit effort at convincing her otherwise which sucks too because I'm an awful liar. How can I try to convince someone else to do something that I, myself, don't even want to do? I can't, but I'm going to have to try to make it seem like I'm trying. How long do I object? Voice my 'opinion'? Can I just say 'Oh, you should probably have it or something' and be done with it? That's almost reinforcing her decision - 'Why would I want to have a kid with a guy that ends all of his sentences with *or something*?'

More effort than that is needed stated in a tone that says 'I give a shit'. How about all of those creepy pictures? That's one thing the pro-life people do well - show a bunch of pics of little dying baby fetuses. If it weren't for those pictures I would view abortion like a trip to the dentist. The pics did me in, them and 15 years of Catholic school.

How long should I pester? How long can I? Like I said before, my feelings are out and about for everyone to see at all times. It's going to be obvious I don't believe in what I'm saying - won't be the first time. Will a couple days work? Or do I need to persuade right up until the doctor goes fishing? The while time I'm thinking 'Please don't listen to me. Please don't listen to me.'.

Does my conscience accept pretending?

"...keeping it."

IV

I just woke up from a couple hours of in and out panic specked with attempts to sleep. I come down the stairs and grab three beers, three so I won't have to get up too much. It's been a day since. I'm sitting on my couch with the remote in my hand and the TV off. My blank stare is just beyond the three beers on the coffee table - one opened, two unopened - into the reflection of the old tube. I feel bad for the TV character. Nobody deserves to be on mid-day television.

Whenever I get up to do something it usually turns into me wandering blindly in circles in a room I didn't intend to be in. It's hard to tell for how long, but if I were a cartoon my foot path would be so worn that the floor would be even with my waist. During this milling my hands make gestures in the air while parts of sentences I never mean to finish leak out of my mouth

"No I..."
"Well..."

Stick me in a mental place right now and I'd never get out.

I open the second of the beers. I try to turn on the TV but the looming question of 'Why?' stops me. This has been a problem. When something terrible happens it's hard to answer that for anything. 'I'll do this... Why? I'll do that... Why?' I don't do this or that, just sit and stare.

I'll get a notebook. I can be like everyone else who gets rich off writing about things that were kinda shitty. I doodle, no pictures or anything. I'm bad at doodling. I write obscene bubble words about myself. **STUPID. MORON. LOST. CHILD.** It's not going to work like this. It's always easier doing this in my head as I'm falling asleep at night. I always think of the greatest ideas for everything at night. My average day is spent thinking up acceptance speeches for awards I haven't won in front of crowds that will never know me. On the last of the three beers - this one to cheers my esteemed colleagues at my lifetime achievement award banquet.

Don't worry... There's more Extra Bold in the fridge.

"Cheers!"

I raise my can, cheers no one and smile. My living room is cluttered and awful. Maybe I'll clean for future guests, but why?

Why is this so bad? Oh yeah, because it's happening and to me. I was going to say, babies aren't that bad, but that's because to this point I could always just get up and leave when it started to be boring or annoying or smelly. What am I going to do? I'm allowed, even allotted, a couple days of mindless self-questioning aren't I? I have to find a real job now. I need to find a place. I need to find a way out of this. There is no way out that I could live with. I need to find a way to deal with this. I need to find some more beers.

I get up and blindly throw the remote to the only place in the room where I'll never find it. Doing loopty loos through the adjoining rooms to the kitchen I wave my hands in a not-so-angry, not-so-upset, not-so-anything way, but rather in a what-the-fuck manner clouded in confusion as to why I'm walking in circles in a room in which nothing I need is in. I manage to reach the kitchen. Took a while being that it only took turning to my left. I think of my hailing critics. I think of why I'm in the kitchen. I think I'm a little sober. I think I need a beer or seven. I think I'll take myself up on that. I open the fridge. After a long deep stare at the mustard I grab the beer - the whole case since there's only 21 left.

I open my eyes and stare at the floor moulding inches from my face. I'm in my room. I made it to my room. I didn't make it to bed, but next to it. I crawl into bed. There are seven empty beer cans on my night stand and floor. There's a half bottle of Jameson accompanying them. Must've had a night. Where did that bottle come from? I'm naked.

I sit up in bed and rub my eyes, yawn a bit too. I feel like shit. I remember my situation. What can only be vomit starts churning in my stomach. Surprisingly it's not as bad as yesterday, a short day's harshness less. Following this trend it will only take about 6871 days to feel completely fine again, give or take a couple. Probably won't work. I feel like shit - physically and emotionally. Never called her yesterday. Told her I needed to have some time to be alone. So what if I chased it with a case of beer and a magic bottle of Jameson. My dealings begin with a text

9:32 - Hey what's up?
9:33 - Nothing what are you up to?
9:40 - Nothing just getting the day started you?
9:41 - Just at work zoning out about everything... How are you feeling?
9:50 - Meh... got stuff out of my system yesterday. Thanks for understanding. How are you feeling?
9:53 - Considering... not too bad. And no problem I needed some alone time as well.
9:54 - Yep.. call me when you get out of work
9:59 - ok

At least I didn't impregnate a giant bitch, quite the opposite actually. I really can't complain about her except maybe her fruitful loins that have had me curled in a ball next to my toilet balling for the last couple days. She, herself, not her fruitful loins, is awesome. We genuinely have a great time around each other, at least before this diaper storm of extreme inconvenience and regret. I think about her, surprisingly outside the realm of thoughts about ways to discretely push her down the stairs. Even if it weren't for the news I could definitely see myself having a baby and eventually marrying her. Too bad this shit had to happen. I think I have to ask her to marry me now. Another time and place and everything could've been perfect.

Cleaning is the thing I do when I want to zone out for a while. It's mindless and accomplishing. I can see what I've done. See results. It's also nice to have the place not smell like chinese food and dip spit. My roommates are slob assholes that never clean up after themselves. I've gotten over it. It's my fault anyway for treating them like adults when they are simple children. I tend to clean the entire downstairs first starting with the kitchen. That's where most of the smells are born. Bleach spray works the best. Makes my eyes burn and lets everyone know what I've done. It goes quick. Not sure why none of my roommates do this ever. Yeah I do - they're awful people. Living room is next. Two garbage bags is usually the number. Some vacuuming as well. Then there's the spitters. It's crucial to be extra careful when throwing out another man's bottle of spit. Haven't thought about my room yet. Probably won't get to it. Anyone who wants to see my room won't care anyway so I'm sure it's fine. I feel good going on two hours but I'm cut short:

1:10 - hey
1:11 - hey what's up
1:13 - nothing just getting out of work you?
1:13 - just cleaning a little wanna come over?
1:15 - yeah... I'm going to take a shower and I'll be over

What am I going to do until then? I just cleaning for an ungodly amount of time. It's going to be at least an hour. What can I do in an hour? I could clean my room. I don't feel like it. I just cleaned the whole house. Can try reading. Everything reminds me of the reason I started cleaning in the first place.

You will all die a gruesome death
Kind of like my life soon to be - dead and gruesome

Life isn't that bad
Life is that bad

I stop reading. It's frustrating and the book sucks. I chuck it to the side and sit there with my head tilted down and eyes looking up staring at anything.

The corner of the ceiling.

The one wall shadowed and the other not but meeting in the middle
My feet and how gross they look.
My feet and how gross they look.
My feet and how gross they look.
My feet and how gross they look.
My feet and how gross my life is
My feet and how shitty my life is.
My feet and my life going to shit
My life and how stupid I am
I am stupid
So so so stupid.

Doorbell

Amazing how zoning on self-pity passes the time.

I run down stairs to open the door. She's standing there with a neutral look on her face. Oh yeah. I'm not in this shit alone. Misery loves company and I'm throwing an end-of-the-century rager. We are going to party like it's 19-you-are-having-a-baby-you-stupid-asshole-and-your-life-is-over.

A 'hi', a hug and a forehead kiss welcomes her through the doorway.

"Wanna go to my room or chill down here?"
"Doesn't matter to me."
"Upstairs it is."

Walking toward the stairs, eventually up, we ignore each other's small talk.

"How was your day?"
"????????? How was yours?"
"?????????"
"That's great how was that?"
"Oh well I killed my neighbor."
"Yeah I had to deal with some shit too."
"I saw a young child crossing the street so I ran it over"
"I had to give an old man medicine and just didn't"
"I jerked off while crushing hamsters in my hands"
"A man fell in front of me and I laughed and kicked him until he threw up because he died"
"I pooped on my own porch."
"I fisted myself while making my schedule for the week"
"I pissed in the orange juice."

We get upstairs and I lay in bed since I have no chairs. She goes to the bathroom. I stare at the ceiling spread out like the Da Vinci dude except with bigger junk. Thinking about nothing. I wait forever. Seems like forever. The one thing I can count on is that forever will never come - at least not soon enough for my liking. Have no choice so I try to relax which is impossible.

She walks out of the bathroom, not avoiding looking at me but definitely not trying to. I don't have a real bed setup. The box spring didn't fit up the stairwell so it's just some plywood on a frame then the mattress. The ply is mid-shin level. You can tell from the marks on mine. She doesn't lay next to me, but rather kind of collapses down trying not to miss the bed completely. She doesn't fail in this attempt. I'm still spread out like a star with my limbs as far apart as possible. She's half on her side facing me with her bottom half front flat on the mattress - knee touching my thigh.

"Why do you have a PBR light on your bed stand?"
"This figure won't maintain itself... and I like the taste of pennies"

She laughs for about a second and a half before she remembers she's pregnant. That's what I assume. That's why I didn't laugh at all. In shitty times you can only laugh for so long. Remembering comes quick followed by feelings of guilt for laughing in the first place. I don't think this is how it's supposed to be. Seems like someone died lately. I guess I have. I laugh for a second and a half thinking about how dramatic I am before I remember why I can't remember the last time I laughed. Guilt follows quickly.

Laughter is the best medicine, but unlike prescription pills that flow like my seed, it comes in a hospital drip - 1.5 to 2 doses only every so often. Mash the button to shit. Doesn't matter.

We haven't gone anywhere. We are still in bed, both staring at the ceiling talking to each other like the other isn't even there. It's been about an hour. I start to wonder if she is just in my head. Is this some terrible neural mix up? Doesn't matter really because my reality is my reality and in my reality I have a really pregnant girlfriend.

She gets up to do something in the bathroom again. Hopefully getting an abortion. Most likely shitting or something. I'm going to have to start changing shitty diapers. That's going to be awful. I hope it's a boy. I'll be over this whole thing by the time it's born. If it's a girl though, I'll be thrown into a 22 year depression always worrying about some guy convincing her that butt sex is actually enjoyable for women. Whether or not he's right isn't the issue here.

She walks back in the room. My head turns solo with a fake half smile. I assume any smile given by a girl to me is fake. The one she gives in return is no outcast to that as she situates her hair to get messed up and crawls next to me - head butting up against my chin. I remember when all I wanted was this - a girl lying next to me, a girl that had nowhere else to be, a girl that didn't want to be anywhere else, a girl that just loved me, a girl that was good enough for me.

How long do people wait to say 'I love you'? A couple days? Weeks? Months? Depends on the people and the situation I assume. I know a bunch that jump from partner to partner, each one a soul-mate because they are 'made for each other'. Some genuinely don't care, or are so indifferent that they'll mirror whatever the other says. Others say it out of a page of their pre-planned 'way things are supposed to go' self-written self-help book.

Date 1 - Nothing
Date 2 - Kiss
Date 3 - Smash
.
.
.
Date 57 - Love

There are the rare few that never say it. They don't need to. They are so nauseatingly cliché that they can feel the other's feelings. Both will hear that they just look happy around each other and both will shrug and think 'Isn't that the point?' They know it and when it's finally said... well duh.

If this is all in my head - her, me, the baby - at least I didn't totally screw myself. No one wants kids, but we are a little older. It's not like we are in high school with any sort of bright future. Neither of those things apply here. We both have degrees in some field we'll never use properly. Neither of us are stupid. I, for some reason, hold myself to a higher standard - not that I've lived up to it but I'd like to think I could some day. Things have changed. Who gives a shit? I do. Time to adjust. I've done it before to certain extents. This one should be a much bigger challenge than anything else. When life changing things happens it sucks. The change overflows into everyday life and overtakes everything. Too late to stop it now. It's a matter of how I'm going to cope.

Wandering in life can be fun. It is fun. Before this, I've been wandering for years, ignoring any sign that would lead to an end. The fun is in the journey type thing. I always figured it would lead to great things. Great things that were hindered by a narrow set of goals. The greatness was supposed to be something unimaginable for me. I never knew what it was. Probably because it was unimaginable.

The years went by and my wandering turned into something else. I was, when I met her, stuck sitting down along my way. My companions were always changing. They would switch like line changes in hockey, except the bench was never ending with an infinite number of people waiting to play. Some even parent-forced into doing so. Players usually never came back for a second shift unless they were really good... at being terrible at life.

In sports only the best stay in for the whole game. I never came out.

I've been so busy avoiding change, fighting every sign of commitment that even hints at throwing me on a path, that I haven't taken one moment to wonder if it's even worth it. It's fun, but I have to build something at some point. I'm fighting the change against something I may not even like. I can't really tell. I don't like being bothered. Whenever I'm not bothered I'm happy. It's a little boring though.

This girl, my baby mama, this change and alteration I've been fighting so hard is my stop, my sub-consciously sought out source of meaning to my close-to-completely-pointless worthlessness. Not sure what I was expecting the end to be. Change seldom comes from doing the same shit every day. I think I was expecting to wake up one morning in a place where I always wanted to be, without any effort or logical maneuver to feasibly be there. Anything I would ever try to change was met with questions.

Why aren't you going out tonight?
Why are you reading?
Why are you clean shaven?
Why are you wearing a shirt with buttons on it?
Why are you banging that girl right now?

Oh yeah. That's how I'm supposed to be. No use in changing now. What was I thinking?

It's sad thinking that it takes a babe, my baby, to make me realize she is what I've been wandering for - for so long. This baby, my career ending knee surgery, my overflowing dam of change I have been standing in front of like a stupid asshole trying to pull a Moses, is a part of what I've always wanted. I hoped that I would be independently wealthy and living in a loft more costly than the entire southern end of my prior home town... but I'm never one for order.

I work fast.

The serious brings out some scholarly thought, or a naive self-banter that keeps me awake at night drowning in some ice cold night sweats. There's no sweat like the sweat of the late night nauseating anxiety flushed type - laying there still as a dead cow in mountain temps but leaking like it's Florida weather.

Convincing myself of anything is never appealing. If it needs convincing then most of the time it shouldn't be - especially feelings for someone. The moment you're forced to rationalize bearing a part of them for the sake of another is the same moment you convince yourself Drain-o is best served with a lime.

It has been a successful trip so far - never rationalizing shit for any reason. No matter what quirky neat little nuance a girl would have, I could rationalize to myself that she wasn't anything special. Half the time I wouldn't even think at all - only assure her she had to leave when her feelings got thrown in with it. She'd laugh and think it cute. I'd laugh and know that that plan just failed. A girl could be as close to perfect as a slight imperfection could get. I'd find something - she's just convenient and there so that's why I'm feeling something here. Nothing to feel here. Go on your way.

Are there others that do this kinda thing? It can't be normal. There wasn't even any traumatic early event for me. I had a shitty high school girlfriend for too long... But who didn't? After that is when I called it quits on the whole couple garbage. Probably shouldn't have gave up on that as a whole based on a ridiculous teenage relationship. I think it worked out to some extent though. I never got anyone pregnant. However, even with all this self-discipline, I may have been falling for her before the awful news.

Now there are too many reasons I have to love her.

On the verge of returning to normalcy I had to plow a fruitful field. Too much to think about now. Thinking about stuff changes it. Instead of knowing how I think, however stupid I know it is, now there's no clue on how to figure out anything - feel stupid for it. Always second guessing myself.

"Whatcha thinkin about?" uninterested but with a job-like obligation to know.

I look at her with confusion, not at what she asked or even what I'm thinking. I know what's in my head. Don't know if I should tell her. I sigh deeply.

"Nothin'."

'Something' is what I need to say. Training myself over the years to avoid discussion has left me a love-cripple. Can't remember the last time I said the words. I can though. Long time ago. It's not a bad thing. Some people are too accustomed to talking that way. Most say it too quickly. They are drowned by the flood of feelings and blind to shortcomings that will eventually ruin everything. Find out a friend gets married and respond "oh that's great you guys have been together for a while" only to find out it's not to the person you're thinking of - it's someone they met a couple weeks ago. It doesn't matter. They are 'in love'. Marriage is a joke and forever is however long you want it to be. *Forever til boredom.*
Yes, these are the ones with weekly soul mates, innately, by the sheer force of nature itself, meant for each and every one. Maybe

you're just a whore?

I don't want to be with someone that says it like the movies - that are so used to it that it's followed by 'pass the salt'. They either say it all the time or don't mean it. If they mean it, if those words are tied to any emotion at all, tricked or true, they should stutter like shit or barely be capable of saying it.

                      Hey....... I....... (giggle) like...... love you.....

An idiot basically.

This is how you judge sincerity. They will also turn red, sweat a lot and probably pick up random things and look at them like they've never seen them before; spoon, napkin, shoe, phone, dildo. Then the thread count in the sheets is a pressing issue.

I don't know if I'm there, but I just might be ready to find out. It's time to think after the fact. See where it takes me. Make a mistake on purpose. This is most definitely a mistake.

Whatever.

Fuck it.

She hugs me, whispers back the same and I squeeze the extra second or two.

The next couple days are filled with less self-pity. I'm not moping around digging my head into the bed with my ass in the air crying and yelling how stupid I am anymore. I'm just digging my head into the bed with my ass in the air because that's how I prefer to sleep. I find myself laughing at things, not immediately interrupted by the thought of the next 18 years haunted by my delayed pelvic reflexes. Water no longer tastes like dirt - found new life in actually cleaning drinking glasses. I missed the nice chlorine taste of the city water. I talk to my roommates for the first time since the other day. Their tones are clues that they probably didn't notice I wasn't around. Things are going back to the regular shit it used to be. Kinda.

I drive around with the windows down, sunglasses on, thinking, not convincing, how life will be just fine. It may not be ideal, but up until now nothing really has been anyway. I act as if it has been some perfect tale of excellence so far. I've had glimpses of perfection, but mostly when I dream or watch successful people on TV. It's sunny and 72 out, slight breeze enough to make my hair look stupid. I wish she wasn't at work right now so we could go do something I wouldn't enjoy otherwise - walk, hike, lay around doing nothing, anything.

I stop at a coffee shop for small food and a coffee. I get out of the car and don't feed the meter. I'm feeling good about today so that terrible, awful, meter bitch can suck a dick. Crossing the street a car flies by almost hitting me. I smile and skip like an ass across the street. Walking up the stairs there is an ugly girl getting ready to leave on the other side of the front glass door. I open it for her with a smile while she ignores me and waddles by. I laugh at what I think is the irony of the situation and head inside.

Eight feet from the counter the hipster cashier asks me what I want. I have no clue. There's no menu anywhere. I'm not sure why they have a menu if they won't let anyone read it. Guess they figure the type of people that come in here already know what they want. I'm no regular coffee house goer. I need things spelled out so others can read the options for me. Don't really care what I get as long as I don't absolutely hate it. Good thing I'm not picky.

"Large coffee... and that"

Pointing to whatever that is behind the glass display. Looks creamy and soft. They give me a number sign (37) thing and suggest I sit down somewhere. Wondering what else I would do I turn around and start to walk through the seating area before giving the selection any real thought. Once through the entire place I find a nice seat half way back next to the front window. I sit.

The wall is especially interesting. This *finding joy in everything* is different for me. There's nothing weighing my throat through my asshole and it's weird. Happiness? I can't tell so I have a small anxiety attack thinking about it. It's funny that the staring spells still apparent. Just realized the hipster girl across the way is getting a little uneasy from me gazing in her direction for what must be a bit. It's hard to avoid - nothing but fixed-gears, tight jeans and other styles from another time and place. It's bearable though - like being trapped in a room with nice accommodations instead of a jail cell with a bald man named Larry.

I stare her way until she flicks me off and leaves. My concentrated lack of concentration snapped by her and the arriving food. I bite into the thing like a starving dog and splash coffee on my face for a chaser. It's hot as shit. My phone buzzes. I burn myself again with the coffee to pass the food down - because I need to have a clear mouth to read and return the text. Before I can read the text I'm distracted by some passing lesbians holding hands. I'm disgusted - not by the gayness, but by the one's flabby ass being held together with some straining spandex. I swig my coffee again and yell 'fuck' louder than I should in public.

12:34 - Thinkin about you... love you

Reading that brings a girlish half-smile to my face. I've been thinking about her too. I text back something of the same with a couple extra jumbled modifiers. I hold the phone in both hands like it's going to run away and never come back. I finish my scone-muffin-pastry-thing, burn the rest of my mouth and head out.

On my way home we text out a play date for tonight. I swerve a lot to avoid accidents. People don't like me. They should be more aware of distracted drivers. You know what they say - a good driver is a 20-something white dude.

At home I busy myself with stuff I can do to music. Time goes by slowly waiting for her. Doesn't help that it's 1 in the afternoon. Why can't she be here now? Because she has a real job that frowns upon weekdays off. I'm bored and tired of pretending to be productive. There's no food. Wish I could wait at her house with all the glorious groceries that women buy themselves. She has healthy stuff too so I wouldn't feel bad about eating 20 yogurts and half a pound of walnuts. Should've just gotten this whole shit over with in high school. Then I could've just moved in with her rich parents, slowly deceived her dad into thinking I'm not such a terrible person, get an upper management position in his office that most if not all others in the company deserve more including the recently hired janitor that gets high in the basement behind a fort of boxes he made while he was training during his first afternoon. I'd be much better off if it went down like that.

Something interrupts my day dream. It's the doorbell. I stop contemplating whether or not the janitor would have a rolling chair in his fort and skip over to the door thinking 'if this is anyone but her I will stab whoever it is'. Peek out the little window at the top of the door and see the top of her head. There's about a hundred locks I have to unlatch because the neighbors across the street enjoy the nice game of 'catch the full bottle of beer that I'm throwing as hard as I can into your house while getting in a late 90's Yukon' a little too often. Excited to get the last one undone I swing the door open faster than normal, almost hitting myself in the face. She jumps in surprise. I catch her in mid air, pull her inside, pin her against the wall and kiss her. Her feet still haven't touched back down. It's a manly feat to keep a girl suspended like that for more than it takes for her to fall, but it's more my whole upper torso crushing her into the wall that's keeping her from going anywhere. She giggles like girls do, probably my gross pregnant man bear is getting too comfortable with her neck. That doesn't make sense but I'm in animal-mode, not think-mode. We part from the wall, her legs now wrapped around my waist as I walk back a few steps into the house. I collapse my legs and gently roll on my back with her on top of me. Now she's straddling me. Not relieving myself as dominator yet I push her left leg and roll to that side. I start gnawing at her clothes in a horn dog attempt to remove them. She gives a half-assed try at stopping me and continues to laugh. I know women - fancy myself a woman-whisperer. So she's probably doing something I could never think of. I get both her hands with my left, needing the right to help my face rip the rest of her clothes off - only a skilled, well-endowed man can lick the clothes off a woman without aid and she's about to remember that I'm neither.

The shedding continues whether she likes it or not - whether she knows it or not. We lay wrestling naked in the entrance, door not even completely closed. I'm busy biting her ass cheek when she says 'stop' in a serious, concerned tone, unlike the usual playful, 'don't actually stop', kind of way.

"Where are your roomates?"
"No clue, why?"
"I can't be naked laying here with them around!"
"Why not?" shoving my head under her arm.
"Because I'm NAKED!"
"Oh yeah... Well I haven't seen any of them in a couple days so they are probably not around or something."
"Well I..."

I can tell she isn't going to stop bitching to me so I roll off, squat next to her, deterring any potential intruder that would happen to come in right now, wrap my arms underneath the appropriate body parts and proceed upstairs. My one real-job-having roommate should be home any second now anyway. My super human horny strength allows me to jump the entire staircase - the hard upwards way. Life isn't bad.

We lay in bed, both sweaty and gross thanks to me. My legs across her stomach, not by choice but rather by adhesion. My hair is shiny and sleek, her's perfect in whatever way it is. don't notice - her eyes have me now. My head is tilted against the wall in an unnoticeably uncomfortable position. There's little talking, just smiles and small kisses indifferent to my condensation on either of us. Her head is in my armpit now.

"Sorry if I smell..."
"I like your smell"

For girls, their own boyfriend's stank is like smelling your own shit; may smell a bit vomit-inducing to others, but to you it's all roses.

"So you're really into us now?" she asks insecure like she's expecting to spit on her butt and peace.

I don't take offense to this knowing that I have second guessed almost every part to every aspect of my life ever since my stupid bitch high school black heart. I laugh mildly.

"Yes I do." forgetting the phrasing of what might've been a question.
"So you're not scared or anything?"
"Scared?! Abso-fuckin-lutely! But more just because I don't know what to expect. We will be fine."
"So you think we are making a good decision?"
"Well yeah..."
"Alright... I love you"

I return the words, shifting my head from the uncomfortable wall to the top of her head - for practicality's sake. I link fingers and do the squeeze with a head kiss. I Squiggle around, not for positioning reason, but rather to make sure this isn't a dream. She wiggles back and I smile wondering what I got myself into - in a good way. I laugh and hold her closer as if she's going to run away. We both start to doze off in a daze, her first though. I have trouble passing out like this. I can feel that she is asleep. Falling off I jerk from the onset of a dream. She's still beside me. That's a start.

I wake up some time later. I see her looking around the room for her clothes. I remind her that I tore them off downstairs. We share a laugh - her's the nervous type thinking I may make her go and get them herself. I put some shorts on and pretend to go downstairs. When I get to the door, instead of leaving, I jump on her, pinning her down to the bed.

"So you want your clothes eh?!"
"YES. I. DO!" in an almost convincing persuasive tone.
"Alright then!"

I tickle her until she can't breath and legit kicks me in the chest. I lose my breath for a second. Laugh it off.

"Don't move!" heading for the door.
"Where would I go?"

I stop short, turn around and stare. I walk back and gently grab her face violently.

"If you're not here when I get back" both laughing like assholes "I will hunt you and chew on your butt until it bleeds!"
"You already do that!"
"Hmmm" and I skip back down the stairs.

Coming down the stairs I get a rare look at one of the roommates. He checks me out, looks at the clothes by the door, back at me and laughs.

"Magenta and green huh?"

Laugh. Instead of explaining I just re-enact what happened - moans, grunts and all. While he laughs it dawns on me, mid hip thrust, that I haven't told him, or anyone about being pregnant. Think I'm ready now, but not this second. I'm picking her clothes up off the floor and she is upstairs. Maybe once she leaves I'll have a chat with my snow leopard of a roommate.

Bring the clothes back. She is under the sheet looking like Aphrodite herself so I throw the clothes over my shoulder and jump in next to her. I finagle my way under the cover so I can rub up on her sweet naked body. She wraps her legs around my waist and holds tight. I have her firm, mid-back and behind her neck. We whisper the shit that others in love say to each other until time passes so quickly she has to go.

Walk her down poking her butt with my feet as we descend. I can hear my roommate still laughing from my performance earlier. I don't blame him, that's the same reaction I get from most girls anyway so I'm used to it. She asks what he's laughing at. He slows and mumbles something about potatoes. She *'hmphs'* and continues to the door. I don't think she was really expecting an answer anyway. At the door we kiss and mumble caring farewells and wishes that we both could stay longer with the other.

Door closes. I turn around and start humping the wall like earlier. Snow leopard laughs.

"So you like her yet?"
"Yes I doooooooo"

I can't say stuff like this in any normal way - makes me feel weird. I either say it in a song or an imitation of a generic goofy-sounding lovey dove. No one is ever quite sure if I'm serious or not except close ones that know I would never joke about it otherwise.

"Sounds serious."
"Yeah she's pregnant" in one brief breath
"Nice" not registering what I said "WHshtat?!"
"Yep.... Full-assed pregnant"
"Dude... That sucks"
"Eh..."
"So what are you guys doing?"
"Uh... like how 'what are we doing'?"
"Are you going to keep it?!"
"Yerp."
"Hmm. Well you shouldn't"
"Yeah... you're probably right"

I sit down on the couch but we don't talk much after this. The TV is on. I chuckle to myself nervously a couple times, reminded of the shitty part of the near future, almost got caught in a dream world for a second there, all lovey-like. I blank out and stare through the TV while my stomach attempts an escape through my throat.

BAHHHHHH!!!!!!!

I fling up in bed, throwing pillows from the nightmare, heart jumping everywhere. I roll violently, still half in a dream. I manage to stop tossing so much and settle down. Wonder what the hell just happened. The post-nightmare calm blesses me with its cold sweaty residue as I look down and see my sweat angel in the sheets

"Holy hell that was a bad one"

I get up to brush my rancid mouth so I can fall back asleep. Looking into the mirror, still brushing my teeth, I'm still in a daze. The reality is slowly beaming back into my head from the eyes of my own reflection. I'm going to be a daddy and my life is over. At least I have something to tell people when asked what I'm doing with my life at the moment (and the next 18 years worth of moments).

'Ruining it' I'll say. That actually won't make any sense since I've already ruined everything. 'What am I doing? Well I have a kid now. Huh? Planned? No. Like most things I just didn't get out of there in time.' That'll be my go to to get people to stop talking to me. My first and last resort.

My teeth are brushed and I lay back down. I remember when staring at the ceiling with panic attacks was only moderately intolerable. Now it brings an even stronger urge to stab myself. Maybe if it wasn't just plain white. Maybe if the ceiling was some color it would distract me in a way that my life wouldn't be so god-awful. Now the humidifier plug is the focus of my unconscious. I remember when I used to humidify my room when she wasn't pregnant. That was nice.

V

(A long, drawn-out tear-filled preamble, followed by...)
"...So I got an abortion..."

The news doesn't suit my suit too well. I go from having a child, accepting a future with a new life, new little person, to a heart sinking crash into a wall of confusion and rage. There are no words. My blank stare doubles as a physical threat. She looks scared. I turn around and pace back and forth going nowhere. She mumbles something but I can't comprehend. My brain has shut off its audible understanding thing. I lean head first on the wall moaning like I got kicked in the head repeatedly by some steel-toed boots. Her hand slides up my back. I have to fight the urge to grab and break it. I walk into the kitchen. She follows saying something. Still can't hear her. I don't want to anyway. I start to scream. It comes out a whompy stutter like when only one window is open in the car.

"Wh(at)?! Wh(y)?! Wh(en)?! Wh(o)?!"

She begins to respond but I tell her to stop. I still don't want to hear from her. Every word is a steel-toe to the temple.

I tell her to leave.
She tries otherwise.
I yell at her to leave.
She starts to cry.

Wasn't expecting any crying for nine months. Especially not from her. I've been psyching myself up for some baby cries. My baby's cries. The baby that's no longer a baby.

I walk to the front door, open it slowly and ask her to leave. Ask me to do something three times and I'll most likely do it. She seems to be no different. She puts her head down and slides her feet outside. On the porch she begins to turn around. I beat her to it - slamming the door before her 180 has a chance. My phone is in hand so I throw it with no governance at whatever is to the right of me while I scream jumbled vulgarities on my way upstairs. I lock myself in my room - I guess in case we get robbed or something because no one ever comes up here - and shove my head in a pillow in an attempt to plow right through it. I can't and I know even if I could nothing would change. The yelling spells are dispersed by vats of silence. The silence is worse than the screams. With the screams brings the goal of ripping my throat apart. The silence brings nothing but reflection. I cough blood onto a pillow and continue.

Maybe, for my own well-being, it's good she didn't ask me. I could barely hold my face straight in support when she first told me we were keeping it. I said the right things but in tones that were completely contradicting. Never wanted a baby. Why the hell would I?" She had to know. She always did have a knack for knowing what I was really feeling. Couldn't even pretend to be interested in half the stuff she told me. She knew. While I was saying those right things, I was showing all the wrong ones - saying 'Yes that's great!' while shaking my head no, flipping her the bird and cocking back with a hay-maker of all hay-makers.

It's like all my other decisions in my life involving others. I never make decisions because I don't want to be held responsible for the outcome. I never wanted to pick out a movie because I was afraid my choice would be bad; not just bad but fucking awful, the kind so fucking awful that you stop watching after 20 minutes. I never picked a place to eat, food's always bad. I would never pick the place to go, the thing to do, times to do it, dates. This situation is no different. Yeah, I didn't spread her legs and let the guy go at it. But I did. I picked the shitty movie, the terrible food, the boring mis-adventure. The only difference is this one makes me want to die.

VI

'm driving on womb US-whatever out of the east and hopefully into the hands of Dr. California. There's nothing back there for me - no debt, no life. It'll be a change. I heard 75 and sunny is a little rough this time of year. I do feel bad about leaving like I did - this morning with no notice to anyone, even myself. If I talked to someone I may have found a reason to stay. I'm easily swayed - little contemplation and much going with the flow. The key to this crux is surrounding myself with nobody but me and I. They all tend to agree and feed off each other's impulsive decision making. Surround yourself with people like you and never feel lonely or isolated again - intellectually stunted maybe, but never isolated. For a trip like this I'll need some reassurance that what I'm doing will be interesting. Wish I put more music on my iPod.

This road sucks, mostly woods and little shit towns. There's a road in California that runs north and south. It's kind of like this one except instead of running through Lady America's sloppy insides, it hugs her curves like a 16-year-old-girl's *going out* dress that makes her dad want to chain her up in the basement, feeding her nothing but donuts and lard in an effort to turn her into some unappealing beast.

I don't know how long my drive will be today. I'm not even sure where this road goes exactly. I just know it ends up in sunny California. If I had to turn but once on this trip, I would end up in Texas, Canadia or right back where I started, maybe a few miles north or south. How long have I been driving anyway? Think I'll stop when I feel safe from disease and inbred rape. Who knows when that'll be. I like this song. Gives me goose bumps.

> Taking the shot. I hit it. Buzzer sounds. The crowd goes bat shit crazy and starts chanting my name. I'm bum-rushed by the rest of the team - all yelling and going temporarily insane. I manage to escape. i run to the court's edge and jump up on the median, pumping my fist with the mob of people trying to touch me. I am a deity of greatness and legend. All eyes are on me
>
> At the after party everyone is congratulating me and throwing me drinks. "YOU WERE AWESOME MAN!" I laugh and

shrug like I do it every day, which I do. Flocks of girls surround me babbling about how great I am and how they want to suck my cock. I say "There's enough of me to go around."

Someone hands me a microphone to make a speech. I grab it and yell "Yo! What's up everyBODDDDYYYYY!?" I get deja vu when everyone erupts like history has repeated. I say thanks to everyone and that we're all getting laid tonight. Someone takes the mic while some blonde twins take hold of both hands.

They drag me upstairs into the master bedroom and throw me down on the king. They start taking off each other's clothes and rubbing up all over. I sit back like it's no big deal. They both start to crawl towards me like two dragons about to eat the shit out of a baby deer.

They are twins but I like the one on the right better. One twin is always better looking than the other. I focus on her for a second. I turn back to the lesser to make sure she's still coming over even though she's not as great. She is now an actual dragon. I'm not surprised but a little turned on. I grab both of them - the blond and the dragon - and start making out. The pillows turn into my kindergarten teacher's massive breasts while the dragon tells me I "don't play the rum successions like you used to." I reply "I gave it up for the good of the mound of the doomed." I turn around and see the monopoly man. He pushes

me out of the way and grabs the
talking dragon by the neck.

"JESUS HELL!!"

I come to coming face to face with a little Asian kid in the passenger seat of an Asian car. I overcompensate and swerve opposite onto the shoulder of the road nearly hitting the rail.

"BAHHH FUCKKK MMEEEE!!"

I continue to violently swerve back and forth with less and less deviation until I finally straighten out enough to stop yelling about fucking myself. Classic daydream into real dream into almost hitting an Asian. The twins get me every time. Why can't the ugly one turn into a hot red head? Or at least a more attractive animal. A dolphin maybe? Shit that wasn't good. God only knows how long I was out. I check the clock. 7:58. It's 7:54. Always set my clock ahead. Allows for time travel.

It's whatever time of the year when it gets dark around this time. I don't think I've driven far enough for a time change so that should be about right, unless it's daylight savings - the dumbest thing ever. It turns back time so it gets dark at 3:30, then turns it forward so it doesn't get dark until midnight. I want to know how it works in Alaska. It's sunny for months at a time there. Instead of hours, it probably skips forward/backwards weeks or months or something. Talk about time travel. I like time travel. I should build a time machine.

I should stop some place. Driving this long I can't really function properly anymore. Mechanically I'm fine. Mentally it's just not there. Any thought turns into a daydream which eventually turns into a real dream which results in almost running over Asians. I slap myself as hard as I can possibly allow myself. I yell "you're going to kill someone if you don't stop somewhere!" I reluctantly agree and look for a place to stop.

Fifteen minutes go by without even a sign that warns of a sign ahead. Meanwhile every tree is turning into a candle on a cake from my whatever-teenth birthday party and the road is taking a detour into the sky where I can see it drop just short of the clouds. I snap out of it for the fact that if I don't I will surely die.

"That doesn't seem too bad at this point." making small talk with myself.

SMACK

I turn the music up to max like I'm driving home drunk at 4AM when it's absolutely necessary. It's the song that gave me the goosebumps however long ago. You know, the one with the shot, the twins, the dragons and Mr. Monopoly??

Before I have a chance to float down another train of chained thought I pull over on the side of the road. If there hasn't been any civilization in this long, they won't mind if I pass out on the side of the road for a few hours. I turn off the car and take a deep breath. Of course now I'm awake. I remember I hid a case of beer from myself in the back so I wouldn't drink and drive. I'm not driving now. Let's celebrate the first day of life.

I reached back and grabbed one. I was trained young to never stop on road trips - pack food, don't drink too much and, if you must, piss in empty Gatorade bottles. The thought of stopping and having to get out of the car is sickening even for a road soda. The one time we went on a trip with my aunt who has the bladder of a horny excited dog. Forty-five minutes into the trip we had to stop. I could feel the tension rise in our car. None of my family went to the bathroom out of principle, maybe because of the filled Gatorade bottles too.

I open the door to a brisk and rejuvenating breeze. It's that time where you're not sure exactly what season it is. One day it's 78 and beautiful - fuck Cali weather. The next it's 43 with a slushy sleet rain - fuck me weather. My sweaty butt steams from my swamp ass as I step out of the car like a wet but warm blanket of embarrassment. Notice the sky walking back to the back. I don't see stars like this much. Google says it only gets better as you go further out west. I open the trunk and find what I've been looking for for such a long minute or two. It's shitty beer but it's in bottles and not so hot.

I twist the cap and tear the shit out of my hand. Not twist off. Lucky I learned at a young age how to open a bottle with just about anything - a matter of leverage and torque. Rustling through some rocks on the side of the road I find a few with an edge that'll suffice. One of them is clean, the others looking like they were shat out of a dragon's asshole. A moment passes while I think of the dragon of my dreams having this up her butt. Seeing that she isn't here, let alone real, I decide to use the clean one. With a finger hooked around the jerry-rigged opener, a slight pull pops the cap. It falls to the ground joining the rubble of the past century.

Sitting on the bumper I stare at the stars - half from desire and half to pretend I'm in a movie at a point where I start getting my shit together. I don't move for a while, except to reach for more beer. The caps are adding up at my feet, eventually telling a story to someone down the line - most likely not though because that someone would have to stop in the exact spot I am right now. I think about the past couple months in a very drunk way - some laughs, some tears, and a lot of confusion as to how and why.

Bottle after bottle is chucked to the side of the road. Sorry Mother Earth but if I get pulled over with that many empties I'm going to be running from more than just a heavy carbon footprint. In a long enough timespan everything is bio-degradable anyway. If that's not true, sorry twice for being such a stupid asshole.

"Alright... Rationalizing with Mother Earth... Time for bed."

The car is cold but I don't care - I have enough things to cover myself with that it doesn't matter. Better than being a thousand degrees hungover. I put the seat back as far as I can - not far since the back is packed with a bunch of random stuff. What I thought would be a quick switch to pass out has turned the opposite and avoids me. Everything is running away. Weird, if everything is running away shouldn't it all be on the same page? It starts to rain. It makes me smile. I used to go out on my parents back porch during thunder storms. I would've laid in the middle of the yard if they'd have let me, but they never did. It would usually be cold so naturally I'd bring a beach towel along to cover myself. Sitting there I would go into some sort of trance - unencumbered by anything except someone asking me what I was doing.

Nothing... I'm doing nothing.

The rain has its habitual effect on me. The beers help too. I've stopped chucking them out the window - wakes me up too much forcing me to get another. There's a half beer in one of the cup holders, an empty in the other.

The sun hits me like the wet washcloth my dad used to wake me up with when I was in grade school which he still denies ever doing. My hand is on a half empty beer in the cup holder. "Run away smarter, not harder." It's really cold in the car - fuck you Cali - so I reach for the keys in the ignition. No keys. I have no idea where they could possibly be. Seeing that I'm living in a car, looking for keys should have been lumped in with the other things left behind.

I get out of the car with my still-cold-from-the-night-frost beer and close the door behind me. Before I throw the bottle into the woods to look for my keys I think *'well... it IS still cold',* and chug the rest before seeing how far into the woods I can get it. I throw my shoulder out trying to crush it as hard as I can against a tree. Amazingly, but not surprisingly, it hits nothing. I turn around and look at the rat maze that is my car - the cheese my keys. If I were me - deliriously and depressingly drunk - where would I hide my keys from myself?

I was too out of it to hide them. I probably left them in or around the case when I got the beer. Go to open the trunk. It's locked. Go back to the front door to get in and pop it. Seeing that nothing has gone terribly wrong yet, the front door is locked as well. A terrifying calm overcomes my general lack of urgency. Well great, a day into my trip and I'm already smashing stuff, would've thought *not until Colorado*. After an initial, still drunk elbow to the driver's side window, I uncharacteristically think of which window I should smash, back right side is now my focus. I walk over to it as if it's my little sister's boyfriend that I found upstairs half naked in her room. Without a third thought about anything I jab my elbow as hard as drunkenly possible.

Holy Christ it hurts.

They don't make windows like they used to, fragile and easily elbow-crushed. I fall against the car and slide down the side, finally resting with my head on the tire. As my bulbous dome plops on the tire I hear a jingle. Christmas comes early nowadays, but it's March, or April and I'm not tripping balls. I roll my pathetic ass over to get up because I can't sit straight up. My face rubs against the tire more than I would like. Shitty things run in streaks - now waiting to get up to see my car is on fire.

During our drunk stint in high school, in fear of getting caught by our parents, my friends and I would often park our drunk asses on random streets so we wouldn't have to go home. We hear a rumor if you're in your car while drunk, even with the car off, you could get a DUI. To avoid this we would always put our keys on the back tire. These experiences should have kicked in before my attempts on the windows, but whatever. I sigh, half with and half at myself. I am a stupid, stupid human being. I swipe the keys off the tire, swing around back, grab three beers - you can't drink all day unless you start in the morning. I saddle up in the driver's seat and head out.

Driving west in the morning is nice. The sun is behind me like I'm running away from something good for me. For a second I forget, or realize I never knew, which direction the sun rises and freak out. I check the car's compass. It says north west. I'm still a little confused, like the times on 695 heading to Baltimore. One second I'm going south, the next I'm going north seeing signs for where I just came from. No way to tell. I go until I see a sign.

By the time a sign shows up I've already forgotten I was worried. West it is. Hurray. They should probably have signs out here saying "You're an idiot! Turn around and go the hell home!" but they don't. Maybe they do. I don't know. Even if they did I would most likely miss them anyway. I'm going west never-the-less. Never. The. Less.

I count time by the number of beers on the passenger side floor. A rough estimate being nine. Around an hour or so. Driving, drinking and smoking cigarettes is one of the most enjoyable things to do as long as you're safe about it. A cigarette is needed to complete the trifecta of stuff that shouldn't be mixed together. My next stop - anywhere that carries smokes. Unfortunately this road is for people like me that hope it will prove modern science wrong and eventually reach the end of a flat earth, hurling me out into the nothingness as if drunk and upset from just nailing an ugly chick - not a lot of room for business. I am lucky though. Everyone needs gas to get there.

I drive a few more beers. It's getting hard to count - bottles stacking up and my vision doubling every so often. I feel like a college co-ed on aderol pulling a string of all-nighters. The road is programmed in my head and goes by with no need of concentration. I forget why I'm here and think of things that make my spine tingle - good and bad. *It's amazing how I can drive like this* I think every beer or two when I snap out of the daydreams. I see the beer in the cup holder and remember I need cigarettes. I look up and of course a gas stop almost passes by. I slam on the breaks without checking behind me as if I want someone to just ram me in the ass. 75 down to 10 in the time it takes to shit yourself. I pull off and park, hammered as shit off of shitty light beer. Hm. Looks like I can pick up some meth while I'm here. I glance back and see my skid marks - a thick diarrhea of rubber joined by a bunch of others. The last hot spot for the never-going-backers.

The place is a real pile of shit. I walk in and it smells like hangover urine. I look around for cashiers and murderers. I cough - half for attention and half out of necessity. After a nervous moment or five a big burly dude comes out of a door. By his looks I can surmise that he has killed something within the last week - animal, human or both.

"What do ya want?" annoyed and homicidal

Don't kill me immediately comes to mind.
Well... Actually... Go for it follows.

"Two packs of non-filters..." whatever "...and a filler upper thing"

He's as confused as I am about the last half of that.

"... and a water."

I hand him forty before he says how much. He hands me three packs. Not seeing a problem with more than I asked for I let it go. I get 21 dollars back. Looking at the change like I thought it'd be free I hand it back to him "for gas." He takes it, puts it in the register and nods. I nod back like a person I know but don't want to say hi to. Turning to walk out, a general fear of everything strikes me. I get outside and wish I had parked the car at the pump. Details like this get people like me killed. Familiar with one of my short-comings I repeat "Actually get the gas you just paid for you stupid asshole!" over and over not to myself, but aloud. I get in and start the car. On my way out I see the pump in my rearview mirror. After slamming on the breaks for a second time I turn around. I get the gas and leave.

The day is an uninterrupted mess of monotony. At one point I find myself lighting my cigarettes off each other in succession. I find fresh air a little boring and obnoxious, at least on this trip at this point. After all, I did get a third pack for the price of each of the first two. At the end of a string of cigs I realize I need a beer. Jesus, beer and tobacco have great sex together. Going 85 and being a strict follower of the family rules of road trips, I attempt to reach back for a beer or seven. Thankfully I had this in mind this morning. The beers are in the back seat but behind me. I can't make it too easy on myself - don't want to get so blasted that I forget to keep going straight. I'm still in control.

I start talking to myself, quickly remembering how annoying boring I am. I need some human interaction, anyone will do. I would even take my burly killer friend from the gas station as long as it would be in public where he has a lesser chance of killing me and getting away with it. Maybe I'll luck out with the next town I cross. Maybe I'll come along an all female bisexual nudist colony - sick of men but welcome to the rare passer-through taking me in like a stray kitten that they want to have sex with for some reason. That would be about a bagillion times better than last night.

This daydream continues, passing time like I'm in love, until I finally hit a town. *Shermantown*. That's a weird name for an all female, bisexual nudist colony. I was thinking I was going to see a big sign saying *Vaginatown* with *We Suck Dick Too!* right under it. Optimism - letting me down since 1986. The speed limit signs slow to 25 as I get closer to the square. I park figuring this place is about 5 square blocks and I can walk to wherever I'm going.

My buzz is wearing off. Bar time.

The highest point I see is in the square, a block off from me. There is definitely a bar there, probably on the higher end though. I don't mind, seeing that the "high point" of this place is two stories above ground. "High end" is probably a High Life and a burger a step above edible. My block walk to the center is quick and brisk. I stand in the middle of the roundabout sharing space with a statue of a guy in uniform. I spin and look for a spot. On the corner is a hotel for fancy-pants that haven't altered-by-scissors most or all of their clothing. The signage is current with the season and matching lights line the letters for a look that looks ok - only a few are out. Across the street and envious is a bank that isn't open. The other corners are filled by undeterminable places that probably shouldn't be there, but for a lack of anything else at all, they are. Hello hotel.

I get to the front doors and swing them open. They are bigger than necessary but not so big that you would notice from a distance farther than fifteen feet. Inside is just like the doors - little bigger than average but nothing special. The ceiling hovers right above where my vertical gets me. The chairs in the lobby are big enough for two to uncomfortably sit together. I think the color scheme is perfect so it's probably uninventive and dated. I look for a lounge sign but find 'Bar This Way'. I go that way.

Walking by the front desk I make eye contact and smile at the mediocre looking girl behind the counter just before she has the time to turn away from disinterest - small town charm. The door to the bar is a normal size and green.

On the other side I run into a wall of smoke. As it seeps into my body through pores and breath I'm reminded that I would like to get some first hand. I dig out the depleted pack and take out the second to last. My lighter is in the car so I walk around unlit like the ads that got me smoking in the first place. That's not true. It was booze, boredom and the inability to not be doing something with my hands at all times.

The room is too big for what it is - a bar for travelers, loners and drunks. Looks like a diner's dining room, the one in the addition on the side of the aluminum trailer. The bar is across the room accompanied by two gentleman and the bartender. It's like a frat boy's first big boy house - a shitty overpriced bar plopped in the kind-of-finished basement with no accompanying furniture. I walk over. The bartender follows me with his eyes, not moving his head. The two guys don't notice/care that I'm joining. They were both born dipping, smoking and drinking. I sit at the far end away from the two who are two seats apart themselves.

"What ya having?"
"Bud bottle and a shot of Jameson... and do you have any matches?"

With no response he turns around, hopefully getting all three. I'll settle for one. Without acknowledging me one of the men slides a lighter down my way. Seeing no other reason I assume it's to me. I nod and thank him. No response. In any other situation it'd be weird. The smoking community, especially the small town type, have their own set of acceptable behaviors. No one likes the ones that bum cigarettes, or even need a lighter, even though everyone has been there at some point. No matter how dedicated a smoker you are you will inevitably be placed in a stranger's graces. Hopefully the good kind. The kind that throw you one every time they light up themselves. This keeps the merry going round. No one likes smoking alone. If you smoke alone you're addicted. If it's a social thing, it's a party. I join the celebration, light up and slide the lighter back across the bar. It falls off seat side.

"Oh shit sorry!" standing to go pick it up.
"I can pick up a damn lighter, sit down!" discouraged but comforted for some reason "Where ya from?"

"Lancaster. It's right out..."
"I know where Lancaster is... Nice town."
"It works."

He still hasn't looked at me and I don't know if I should keep talking. He probably hasn't noticed that he's talking to me. I guess he had to have heard. He likes Lancaster. I wouldn't have listened to me. I'm me and I try to ignore most of the things I say. I can't repeat half the things I say. I don't pay any attention.

Do I ever say anything?
When was the last time I've said something?

Oh shit sorry...

Right.

The bartender has my beer and shot. No matches. Doesn't matter. Good teamwork.

"Hell you doin out here?"
"Uhh..." scrambling for an answer "Getting away for a bit."
"What happened?" indifferent and to the point.
Debating with myself, "Uhhh... Got a girl pregnant, hated it, fell in love, loved it then an unexpected abortion, kinda went... am going crazy so I started driving."
"...Lucky..."

The bartender laughs, no intention of hiding. I stare blankly at the bar with a contemplating *huh* and rip the shit out of the shot that's been sitting there for a little too long. Feels warm but gives me a chill. That one went down nice. Amazing how Jameson can cross such a spectrum of reactions from a smile to a vomit. I look like an idiot when I smile. Looking like an idiot my eyes are just above the bar pointing at nothing in particular. I zone out a bit like I'm driving. I think about things, laugh noticeably and shake my head at how stupid I must look.

"Good point"

The rest of the time here follows similarly. There are more beers than words and more shots than beers. The man isn't excited about talking to me, but doesn't mind either. He shares some stories of his own. He still hasn't looked at me. I try to listen and relate with irrelevant experiences. I put more effort into not slurring than any pertinent contribution. Time goes by like it usually does, unnoticed. Last call comes along with confusion on my part as to what time it is. I get my tab and it's cheap as shit. I tip 57%. Should tell my friends about this place. My indifferent friend asks me for a cigarette. I realize I haven't ripped one since that first. Uncharacteristic of me.

Usually this kind of place would have me lighting cigs off each other. I take out the pack and there's one left. He notices and says

"Nevermind."
"Bah!" Waving my hands in disagreement "Have it! I don't need it anyway."
"Really?" looking me in the eyes "Thanks."
"One drag though."
"Absolutely"

After the drag I say bye and thanks. He looks confused about what I'm thanking him for but doesn't bother asking. I walk back into the slightly above average lobby looking for the hot desk clerk to check in. She's not there. No bell. Drunk and tired I lean over the counter, feet in the air and look for something to make noise with. Hoping for something ridiculous like a bull horn, I find the bell I was looking for. I place it where I think it should be and tap it to an annoying rhythm. There's a door behind the desk and I can hear something rustling on the other side. The lady comes out looking annoyed. It's probably my sense of rhythm, my timing or both that has her up in a huff.

"Check in ain't 'til 5."
"Ok... Then why are you sleeping back there?"
"To make sure everything is ok down here."
"But everything *ISN'T* ok down here!"
"What's wrong?"
"I need to check in and I gave away my last cigarette!"
"Well, there's no check in right now."
"You're pretty"
"What?"
"How bout there is check in now?"
"Are you high?"
"High on your butt..." trying to wink but blinking both eyes with severe emphasis instead.

She laughs.

"You are fucked up aren't you?"
"I did give my last cigarette away..."

She laughs again and shakes her head with an appropriate emotion that slips my mind right now. She turns and goes back into the back room - shitshitshit- but doesn't close the door - yesyesyes. I hear rustling - she's a rustler. As I'm about to walk around the desk to go have sex with her she returns with a pack of cigarettes. Perfect - wanted cigarettes more than the room anyway. She hands me a cigarette and asks me what I'm doing.

"Just wonderinnn whatcha doooin.... EW GROSS MENTHOL?!"
"Don't want it?" reaching to get it back

"Didn't say that." flailing backwards.

She breaks out a zippo and waves the flame in front of my face. I lean in to oblige and miss, almost lighting my eyebrows on fire. I swipe it and mumble 'shwomen can't lshlit brbl eye not safe' and spend a few seconds lighting it myself. I inhale. It tickles so I laugh and blow the smoke directly in her face. She coughs and turns away as I slur an apology with a smile. She comes back around with a key in her hand.

"Give me your wallet."
"Give me your underwear."
"No, so ya have ta come back in the morning ya drunk ass."
"Oh yeah... that."
127.   Down the hall on your right."

She points me to the hall. I stare where she's pointing and ask "There?" pointing to the same hallway.

"Yes."
"Cool. Can you show me?"
"Show you what?"
"Where the hall goes."
"It goes to your room now get."
"Get what?"
"Get the hell down the hall ya mess."
"You're a mess."

She goes back into her room yelling "get goin" as she slams the door behind her.

I walk to the hall.
I walk down the hall.
The hall is long.
119
120
Almost there.
128
129
I check the number on the key.
I turn around
128
127
There.

The key is one of those old fashioned keys where it's an actual key. I've never been good with them. I've always found myself stuck on porches to the places I've had keys to. Technology isn't for me. I try and have trouble: can't get it in, once it is in I can't turn it, I turn it but lock it more. I get angry and kick the door with my toe and smack the doorknob while barking. Frustration doesn't work so I try apathy. The doorknob twists and I'm in. I get just beyond the swing of the door before collapsing on the ground. I should've given the lady money for butt. Would've probably been a waste.

I wake up to some banging on a door I don't remember opening in a room I don't remember seeing. I get up and notice the bed I could've slept in if I made it another four steps. Guess I have my reasons. My head hurts. Feels like I opened the door by jumping head first through it. My stomach feels like a plastic handle of vodka. The banging continues despite me thinking of the other things. I get up and look through the peep hole like I may not open it pending who it is. Unless it's someone wielding an axe I'll probably open it. Although an axe to the forehead might be a relief. It's an old ugly woman holding what could be my wallet, or anyone else's in the world - brown and lame. I open the door.

"Here's ya wallet."

Last night slowly leaks back into my head - the hotel, the lounge/bar, the local, the booze, the hostess lady thing situation. I'm supposed to have the key aren't I? That's why she has my wallet. So yes. Where's the key? It isn't anywhere - not in my pockets or any of the square foot of floor I preferred for my bed last night. This can't be good. Losing one of those credit card keys in normal hotels is fine. Whenever I visit I usually have to get three or four rounds of them at the desk because I forget to pick them up leaving the room. Losing a key like this involves a set of new locks - money I didn't put in my impromptu budget running out the door. Should always know to put in the *lost real key at the hotel with slightly above average sized doors with the guy at the bar that smokes cigarettes who you regrettably gave your last to.* It's common sense really.

"Thanks.. Um... I don't know where the key is... It should be somewhere in this area. I don't know what happened."
"Well I would normally have your legs broke. Lucky fer you your drunk ass left it in the hole."
"Oh." Relieved "yeah, I've been having trouble with that lately."

Seemingly confused she rolls her eyes, hands me the wallet and walks away muttering something about 'irresponsible mess'. If she's muttering at me she could've just muttered to my face. I wouldn't have been insulted. 'Irresponsible mess' is a bit of an upgrade right now. Did I pay for the room? Did I just get the *drunk bum special* - feels so bad she just let me stay. Not too worried about it. With not losing the key and no room charge I think I made money stopping in here.

"Phone. Wallet. Keys." padding each spot they should most likely be "yup."

I walk down the hall and into the lobby area. It's quiet. I see my lady friend helping some guests.

"Thanks again BYYEEEEE!!"

Seeing the few around her turn around like I just shot a gun into the ceiling I realize that the deafening silence is just in my head and that I yelled pretty loud. The people are old and naturally disgusted with me immediately. My lady friend shakes her head with a slight grin like a mother at a son who just did something embarrassingly stupid but forgivably funny. She waves without looking as I open the just-above-average front doors.

It's sunny as shit outside. Very unpleasant right away. I fall backwards a little as if my body is covered with eyes.

"BAH!"

That's one way to save money - appear so pathetic that someone feels the need to take care of you. It's easy when it's true. I feel kinda bad since I do have money. But then again, who knows how much I will need on this trip. Don't know how long it will even take. I'm probably going the wrong way - have to take that into consideration. A lonely drunk road trip tends to warrant spontaneity as well as stupidity. Both are at a cost - sometimes money, sometimes the clap. I feel homeless. I am homeless. No I'm not. Oh shit maybe I am - I never set up rent or someone to take my spot. Oh well my roommates were complete assholes anyway.

It's hot as shit. I should take off my jacket.

I don't.

I get lost on the way back to the car. I'm not in a hurry so I'm not upset - allows me to see the scenery of good old wherever I am. I hope I turn the right way on my road. I have trouble with directions at this time of day, whatever that it is. I'm a block off where I was and I can hear the banjos playing. I turn around and run back to the hotel. I see the car two blocks away. I can tell it's mine from the lost wheel flare - a result of my dad plus Thanksgiving antics.

I start walking.

There's a place that sells coffee. I would call it a coffee shop, but it's not. They only have small. I count mentally how many cup holders I have in the car - four. I buy four cups of coffee and four packs of cigarettes and for a second forget that I'm by myself.

VII

This drive really blows. Why couldn't my parents be cool and have raised me in California. I could have had my experience there and wanted to go to sad-assed, rain-all-the-time Seattle. Driving up the coast with beaches and bitches waving hi would sure be a bunch better than these shit-assed woods filled with hermits - none I imagine being blonde, attractive or a preference for butt-play. Not sure why I'm thinking about women. It's like I'm on a treadmill with a rolling scenery machine next to me except if I stop now I can't go look up porn, jerk off and fall asleep. If I stop now it would be up to imagination. Even if I happen to see a random willing woman on the side of the road, I would most likely not be able to get it going. If you ever want to kill a boner, think about a dead baby - your dead baby.

The four cups of coffee are empty now collected with the beer bottles on the passenger side floor. There's a few unopened. I lean over to pick one up, completely blind to the road for a good 20 seconds as I fumble around the full ones that are on the farther side of close.

Beer holds my attention for a few before I add chain smoking cigarettes. God I'm annoying. How many more miles? I estimate somewhere around a lot more than I would prefer. I'm looking around the car frantically for something to occupy my time. Shit. The coffee, booze and cigarettes result in a concentrated lack of concentration toward everything. I skip from thing to thing to thing to thing to thing to thing thing to thing tiong thinawwe gn. A receipt! Twenty on twelve is good. She or he probably wanted to really sleep with me after that. A CD I haven't listened to in a while. I put it in the CD player because that's where they go "HAHA!" This CD sucks. I throw it out the window. My car is dirty. I throw garbage in the back. My car is clean! I find a plastic bag and wrap it around the shifter for future garbage. What's-her-face saw me do that once. She didn't understand why I wouldn't just take the garbage out with me once I would eventually stop and get out. I chuckled and thought of ways to kill her. Look, a TREE!

"Well hello tree... I see you are tall and prosperous through these parts."
"Why yes sir. I technically am having sex constantly. Life is grand."
"Good to hear tree... I may not technically be having sex constantly but life is grand as well."
"Why so grand?"
"Because I'm running away from my problems and probably will never go back because I'm a coward."
"Very good. Very good."
"Yes. Yes. I have to agree."

Flagging myself, I dump the rest of my fourth beer out the window and put it in my new garbage bag. I light a cig with a deep breath of '*Jesus what the shit*' and stare straight, not at the road, but at my slight reflection in the windshield. Try staring yourself in the eyes through glass. You'll see a lot about yourself. You will eventually start talking to yourself and confessing stuff. It helps if you are super drunk and stoned in between vomit episodes. I saw this coming. Inevitable talking to myself through made up characters from the scenery. For how tall and grand the tree was, didn't really help much. Last time I bare my soul to such a grand tree.

I'm glad I did not get a fifth cup of coffee. I may have had a heart attack. I would not mind dying but the guy who sold it to me might have had a lawsuit to burden him if I would have had survived this hypothetical situation. He would not have had anything to worry about since I would have had been too pissed about not dying to think of him. If anything I would have had gone back and asked him to kill me himself. Wonder what tense *would have had* is. Probably perfect preterit past perfect.

Fuckin shit!

Fuck Cali... How far is the next town?

I speed up to just under dangerous in an effort to rid myself of me. I picture my new alter egos and states of mind drifting behind me. They are ghost like and can float through doors, walls and do pretty much anything else, except exceed the speed limit.

Ever think about what you are thinking and think '*God I'm lonely!*'...? I don't. For me it is calmly '*I need help...*'

The next town is somewhere between *not close enough* and *where am I going*. Crank the commercials that have been playing on the radio, light another bogue off the one in my mouth, speed up to just above dangerous and black out for the duration... where am I going?

I come to a town just like the last one - square block of stuff which is not that great and surrounded by a bunch of other stuff that's not too great either. May have got turned around. Not quite sure how that's possible driving straight. I have done dumber things before. But still, how is that possible? How is shitting three times in 20 minutes possible? My mother, that's how - she fed me juice instead of food for a year about. I have trouble with anything but cheese. No clear liquids or above average juicy fruits or else I am running in jeans. Wonder what mom is doing. I smack myself and get back on track - my long, straight, going nowhere track. Wonder if I am going to win this meet. It's not a sprint. I have the endurance and the ability to put myself in better places than where I am right now.

Jesus shit! I need some human interaction.

The next stop comes and seems less populated than a turnpike rest stop. Exit is a mile away so I speed up to gain 15 seconds of time to do nothing. Off the exit about 100 feet I am right in the middle of town. No point in drawing it out. If it were not this way I would drive straight off the exit back onto the road thing. Instead I park at the first spot and get out. I pick my boxers out of my asshole. Those two have become too acquainted in the past couple hours. There's a half full beer on the passenger seat. Can't have that. I walk fast like I know where I'm going, like when I am with people in an unfamiliar city - always start walking to find out my friends are a block the other direction and I am going the wrong way - with the now quarter full beer. This also applies to driving, my sentences, life decisions, relationships and anything else that presents the possibility of responsibility. The great part of not knowing where I am going or what I am doing is that there is no right or wrong, just new. I come to a dead end with nothing around. Looking for people, I throw my empty beer as far as I feel like - underhand about 4 feet from mine. A dead end, predictable - pay too little attention to myself, or too much. Not sure. I do know if I keep thinking like this I will end up in the middle of the dead end nothingness. On my way into that nothingness I turn around and possibly head in the right direction.

This town is not that bad. It is a little better than the last one in that it knows what it is. It's not trying to be something it's not. There is no reason to think this except that I have not seen unnecessarily, slightly over-sized doors to something yet. Eh, maybe I do. Walking closer to the heart of the place I notice the streets are a little nicer. There are nice stores with nice fronts - the kinda stores that I would go in with a girl that didn't kill our unborn child. I would pretend to look at stuff and end up in the women section. She would laugh and I would do something stupid only she would think funny, preserving her smile just a little longer. From her non-baby-killing smile I would smile my stupid smile, my real smile, the smile that you get when you find or figure out that the girl you like likes you too... and won't murder your babies....%!.8$

I need help

This would normally build on itself but I realize I've needed to pee for a while now. My balls feel like two grapefruits almost forcing me to uncontrollably piss out my butt. That will come later. My bladder no longer feels enclosed, rather a gallon bowl filled with urine that for some reason is teetering on a counter's edge - the kids sit and watch instead of moving it back. I start pee running - a soft run with no contact points. An abrasive impact would cause the bowl to topple over. I look like the old Olympians in the dumber-than-curling event of *speed walking* - hips swerving like a porn star sitting on a dildo plugged onto the floor. The great thing about having to piss real bad is that I don't have to *shit* real bad. Haven't shit in a bit. I am going to have to shit. By the time I find a bathroom I won't be able to stand up, might as well shit anyway.

Shit.

Gotta shit.

I'm frantically running like I have to shit and piss. I would describe it differently, but this is the way I describe idiots who look like assholes when they run. Idiot-like and in desperate need of a toilet I see a general store across the street. Cupping my balls and pinching my butt I pick up the pace. I am going to shit myself. Across the street I step up on the side walk, legs bending a little more to prevent my butt region from pulsing.

Avoid impact moments.

Open the door.

Spot the cashier.

"Where's your bathroom?" in a forced relaxed tone, like when you know you are going to kill someone but want to make sure they deserve it before you do.

"Customers only"

I reach in my back pocket, grab my wallet, throw it at his face and start running towards the back.

"Where am I going?!" hands like a vice on my cheeks.
"Back to the right... What do you want?"
"GUM!"
"What kind?"
"Spearmint." sprinting back and to the right - would take odds on if it's occupied or not, but there are no odds. It will be occupied.
"You have to spend at least a dollar!"
"And whatever else!"

Get to the door and shake the knob violently.

Locked.

I am surprised... that I tried.

"One second!" from a stranger I would murder if I didn't mind shitting myself

A normal person with normal bowels normally would believe this. Being an abnormal person with abnormal bowels I normally don't believe this and that's because I know it's a lie. When I yell 'one sec' I laugh to myself while playing games on my phone wondering if my other leg will fall asleep before I'm done thinking *that poor bastard is going to shit himself outside that very door.* This poor bastard is wishing karma wasn't such an awful bitch right now because I'm going to shit myself right outside this very door. My knob shake gives it away. Whoever is in there is shitting and thanking Christ that he/she is not me right now, laughing with empathy. That bastard or bitch. I'm bent over like I got stabbed in the stomach. I start counting, not seconds, not minutes or anything else. I'm not really counting. I'm just groaning in succession. This is about the time I come to terms with the situation, like I'm on my deathbed with a priest absolving me of all the shitty shit I've done in my life.

Well...

I am going to shit myself in public.

Again.

I start drafting a deal. A deal proposed to God and the Devil. A deal that will involve me not shitting myself with clauses built in in regards to the potential and inevitable situation where I do in fact shit myself. These will focus more on the exact amount of shitting myself that will go on - little run down the leg, maybe even contained in my boxers if one of them happen to be day drinking and overly generous. I prefer God to the Devil. God will forgive me when I eventually fall short on my side of the bargain. The key is to put in a bunch of modifiers - 'I will *try* to got to Church every Sunday' 'I *may* never have premarital sex with my girlfriend, but *if* I happen to I will *make an effort* to not sodomize her.' *Trying* means I'll set an alarm that I will have to get up and turn off immediately. *May* means as long as the opportunity doesn't present itself I may have a chance of abstaining. *Make an effort* means that there will be no real effort put forth to stop myself from doing anything. The Devil is more malevolent than God. He'll trick pretty easily and end up with my soul. I got no fiddle, couldn't play one if I did.

Looking for things to shit in within grasp, the door swings open. My eyes are blurred from oncoming tears but I swear to myself I see some blond and some nice cleavage. Fantastic, I arrived in a town of trannies. Rolling in I take a whiff of the room to check how bad. I have always done this. Habit or something. Have to know how bad. It's not bad. It's covered with the floral soap - the same soap the Y used to have (probably still does) for its shower room - so it doesn't matter, not that it would otherwise. That she-he bitch-bastard washed its hands while I was out there finding a box to shit in. Doesn't matter now. I'm half naked and the door isn't closed.

It's not so much a push but a release.

Relief.

No wonder everyone wants to have sex with me.

Sometime later, breathing a deep whiff of what used to be me, I get up and get myself together, always a concern. Never know what kind of mess is mucking up everything down there. I usually do not wash my hand, but now is an exception. Lathering, I check myself out in the mirror. I am sweating and flushed in my complexion. I'm not flushed with shit so it doesn't bother me. I rinse my hands and dry them, not too much. I like to have a little soap-wet to rub the back of my pants with just in case I missed a hot spot. My sense of smell is lame at best. Think I'm ready to get out of here. I open the door to face this shit town.

Walking out and down an aisle I notice a blond girl doing pricing stuff with a smile. She cannot be smiling about pricing. She must be holding back laughter, most likely directed at me. She peeks. We make indirect eye contact. She attempts to hide her hilarity even more as I laugh, shrug my shoulders and try to say something funny that comes out as mumbled jumbled gibberish. My speech isn't a result of her knowing I just bombed the back half of the store, but more from the intimidation I feel from anyone slightly attractive. However, I can usually flip this feeling into something cute and adorable. This time might be an exception seeing that I recently let loose a sewer of spoiled egg and methane just paces away. I'm passed her now. Imagine that the floral essence cover from my hand swipe on my ass has gone and she may be in some trouble now. I peek back and we make indirect eye contact. She isn't smiling anymore.

Should've lit a match.

Half way down the block I hear someone screaming. Their screams come closer and closer. Assuming I accidentally stole something I continue like I didn't. After a moment or three a guy gently grabs me on the shoulder. It's the guy from the store with the bathroom. He's all out of breath. I pride myself on speed-walking to nowhere special. I greet him in an inconspicuous manner like I do everyone else - adults, children, men, women... animals when I'm drunk:

"Well hey.... Whaaat's up?"

Vacant of breath he just hands me a small package. It's a pack of spearmint gum, greeting cards, my wallet and 35 cents change.

"You look out of town. Figured you could send somethin' home."

"Oh... yeah that's a possibility."
"We don't have post cards. No one chooses to come here for the most part. No point"
"Naaah it's fine..." sympathetically laughing trying to make him feel better about being willing to admit to a complete stranger that no one ever wants to come here. "...I came didn't I?"

Nodding and waving in place of words he turns around and shuffles slow back to the store, hopefully for him to slam the little blond girl in that rancid bathroom of theirs. I can't remember what she looks like, even if she's cute or not. Looking at the gum, greeting cards and change I remember that I had to buy something, a toll to shit. I would've rather him keep the five and not remind me that I had that money in the first place. He did mean well though. It's a draw in my head whether or not I would nod to the dude if I ever see him again. I'll probably puss out and nod, even make a comment about the greeting cards. He could have bought a candy bar or something. I'm starving.

Nothing to do. The hotel is probably where it was in the last town, in the middle. I don't really want to go yet. It's not dark. What day is it? Wonder if a younger crowd goes out on these nights. Wonder if there is a younger crowd. That blond girl seemed young. She is probably 12. She must've been older since she know the smell of shit. Girls learn that sort of thing when they mature and hang out with more and more guys. They themselves only shit roses and fairy tales. Let's shoot for 18. Towns like this never care about the legalities of youngsters and drinking. Guess I should check in the hotel. I'm pretty sure it's someone's job at every hotel to know the *goins ons*'s of the local nightlife, even if it is for a random runaway mid-twenty-something's chasing a night on the three-square-blocks.

I find the hotel blablabla actually pay blablabla hit on an old woman blablabla and run into my room for the second half of the brown bowl. It would be great if it was the second half with that younger blond's butt that I saw earlier. Not that I don't enjoy diarrhea, I do, but I would like some cuddling after the fact. Some naked laying around maybe? Isn't that what we all want? Guess some would be happy with regular bowel movements. I am as long as I'm within an eye-fuck of a bathroom. If not, turns out ugly... and smelly.

I'm getting settled. The handful of clothes I grabbed from the car is carefully thrown on the desk in the corner. In an effort to compete with other hotels in big interesting cities this place has put in a really complicated shower faucet. Push, pull, turn, twist, yank, yell at, neglect, spank... nothing works. I call the front desk naked in the other room with my balls in my off hand. They tell me not to worry and that many people have this problem. I make a face she can't see because she's on the phone and that's impossible for a majority of people. If I didn't already pay, I would leave right now. It's one of those push-twist-pull ones. O yeah. The water is freezing cold. I assume I won't figure out how to make it warm so I jump in and scream like 4th grade girls in a screaming competition during recess. Soap the head, soap the feet, soap the head, soap the pits. The essentials are all I can stand so I rinse and get out. While turning it off the water gets hot. I leave it on, get dressed and leave.

The old lady at the front seems promising. For what I do not know.

"Well hello... Whaaat's up?"
"Hello" visibly confused.
"Where's the party tonight?!"
"What party?" even more confused.
"Where can I go to find people like me?!"
"Oh my! I'm sorry... I'm getting old... You can pretty much anywhere."
"Really?"
"Yes... There's almost no Puerto Ricans here."
"Ahhh..." sort of racist but I did have a run in with a pack of them once. Got over it though when my buddy who was with me finally admitted to throwing something at their car while we were walking by.
"Thanks, but I was thinking like *where can I get laid,* or something along those lines."
"Oh my! I guess McSwanson's down the street"
"Thanks" visibly confused but lost on her.

She points that way.

I point at her,

Say *thanks* again,

and leave without taking notice to the way she pointed.

McSwanson's is deceiving like a warehouse in the middle of New York, not that I've ever been - very small, shitty looking entrance, but inside a great... warehouse. It's like this town was about to explode into a thriving metropolis and some rich asshole built this place thinking he thought it through enough. Then everyone remembered they were in the middle of nowhere and all moved away, leaving this stupid place standing like a giant among children. A giant with children is not good - big stuff with small stuff. Even though the place where this place is completely blows, I can see where the guy was coming from.

On the other side of the door it's a little crowded. There are people like me everywhere - young and, to the credit of the desk lady, not Puerto Rican. They are all early twenties, in college of some sort, eagerly waiting to escape this hole they will later realize they never want to leave. For now they play in this safe haven of booze, familiarity and potential for heterosexual sodomy, maybe even some gay shit too. It's college. Now's the acceptable time to blame it on your drunk.

The ceiling is high, but filled with nooks and other places to hide. The bar is across the way past a couple stoops and lounging areas. It's about half full - half girls and half dudes. It's early so it's still a 5th grade cafeteria. There is a row of three empty seat. I make an ordeal of sitting down, situating myself a few times and throwing my pocket stuff everywhere while thinking of something Johnny Depp would drink to order. Maybe I can start some conversation. The soon to be regardlessly hot bartender sees me and asks what I'm having.

"Jameson."

Shit. She snuck up on me too fast, no time to think. Jameson's not a conversation starter at all. These parts remind me of the Catholic coal regions - guys love the stuff, girls... actually not sure, not many up there. Few girls like Jameson. The ones that do usually get completely black out smashed. This wouldn't be a bad thing for the night, good even. However, the last thing I need is some stupid girl crying rape because she can't remember how all over me she was the night before while I'm running out of town with my pants on my head and her thong on my balls. Consciously avoiding that would be a plus for this whole trip. This town doesn't seem like the type to throw outsiders in jail so much as take them out back and shoot them with a shotgun while drinking a Bud pounder.

My drink comes on the rocks. Didn't think about how it was coming. Usually a shot, but I'm not complaining. I'm just happy I didn't choke and vomit when she asked. I can pretend it's something worthy of self-introduction. Not being too late in the game - me semi-shirtless with a flamboyant hand mid chest gest during a rant about how the *Life is Good* franchise is a mockery of Jimmy Buffet's line *Be As You Are* - I feel comfortable asking the bartender her name. If I asked any later she would assume I was hitting on her.

I ask.
She says.
I don't listen.

We talk like me and my friend from the last town except I stare at her chest a lot more. She asks me the out-of-towner questions. Having no interest in myself I give short, uninteresting answers. I ask her about her and continue not listening. She probably has figured out I'm not listening, but at least I'm not hitting on her. This works better anyway. Disenchanted with the rest of her forced company, she continues talking to me, or maybe it's the beard I just noticed I have in the mirror behind the bar that's been sharing time with the bartender's boobs.

My glass is empty. She sees and replaces it before I can tell her otherwise. Why drink the special when you can drink whiskey for three times as much? She keeps prodding me with questions. A little aggressive now. I think she's hitting on me now. I think I'm drunk now. Slipping into old ways is easy when they haven't changed. Lack of eye contact and friendly insults that are borderline inappropriate for the most part should work if I remember correctly - think about it too much and I'm already lost.

Not impressed with my first three answers to *why the hell are you out here?* (because., where? and what?) she asks again.

"So why the hell are you out here?"
"Well... It's a funny story..." all drunk already somehow, subtly laughing "ABORTION!"

She's confused. Everyone is always confused around me around here. I smile with frowning eyes, tilt my head a little to the side and glare above her head to the same side my head is tilting. I'm drunk to the point now where I can't tell if I'm serious or if I'm enjoying acting like I'm on T.V. I don't like acting though. Some weird jumbled shit. I temporarily black out thinking of unrelated things like how I may be addicted to coffee and how stupid crayons are.

Not upset.

One of the girls next to me is staring over my way waiting to make eye contact.

Sorry dear this is against my rules.

"Hey."

So much for that rule.

Taken off guard she chokes and for a half sec I think to myself *please throw up*. She doesn't. Instead she introduces herself. I don't listen and introduce myself. She doesn't waste time and dives into my life. She's one of the abrasive ones, strong and over confident. She takes pride in being able to talk about touchy subjects in a *matter of fact* tone. The type that will break down if poked right, but not in public. Should be fun.

"So abortion?"
"Not me."
"No shit... who is she?"
"My dead baby's mama."

She catches herself from laughing out loud (LOLing). My neutral level of respect I give everyone when I meet them drops because that wasn't funny. It wasn't a one liner. It was more of a running joke in a sitcom. If I were in one, *dead baby mama* would be what my friends would call whats-her-face for the half season we would be on the air - running enough to almost be worthy of a *hymph* from the diehard fans that will *have no idea why they canceled that show when they have this shit on* while watching that shit.

"It's ok.. I only tricked myself into loving her anyway."
"How's that possible?"
"You can rationalize any shitty situation... a sign, fate, a nudge from God, *it could be a lot worse...*"
"Well that's a good quality."
"Yeah... until the sign leads to a dead end. Fate forever unsatisfied. The nudge from God is actually your drunk friend pushing you to talk to a girl who later you'll find out has herpes and then the next ten years *could've been worse* at best."
"You have herpes?"

I laugh. She laughs one of those *so-what-get-over-it-wait-but-seriously-do-you-have-herpes* laugh. They are always good to be around, not that I'm under it right now. Maybe I am. All bad things are associated with some sort of denial - *she's not dead, she does like me, they must've mixed up my test with someone else's.*

"No... happened to a friend."
"Suuuurrrreeeeee"
"I got papers!"
"I'm sure you do..."

This blabber chit chat goes back and forth for a while. We get more drinks, lots of shots. We get smashed and do things that smashed people do - yell, make a scene, order more shots. She's hot I think/don't care. I reach into my pocket to fix my smooshed junk. It'd be less obvious if I unbuttoned my pants and punish myself. The greeting cards are still in my pocket, perfect. I laugh knowing that this girl is now going to come back to the hotel with me. I find a pen and write *leave with me? Check Yes or Absolutely* on one of the cards and slide it over. She looks and laughs and starts writing something. She slides it back to me. She made another box with *no* beside it and checked it. I laugh loudly again. This should be a fun night.

Half a moment later I feel her take hold of my hand and shove it in between something warm. I'm still not really looking at her too too much so I guess what it is. I look and it's not. It's her arm pit. Thank the good bearer of good news - thought it was a little stubbly. She gets up still holding some part of my arm and drags me out. I say 'wait I need to pay my tab!' but she explains they will grat' it automatically. Good for me since whatever they charge is probably less than what I'd tip them anyway.

"Phone, wallet, keys?" tapping the places where they should be
"Yep."

Before I turn back to her I spot her friends looking pissed and confused - not a surprise for either. She did ignore them all night and about to leave with the sexiest dude in this high-ceilinged shit hole. They spy us and start walking just under run-speed after us as if I'm dragging her to some rape van. I wish they would get it right - it's a rape Jeep Liberty. I turn back to her...

"GO!GO!GO!GO!"

She tightens her already circulation-killing grip and drags me out the door, almost hitting me with such. Out the entrance and into the place next door, a coffee shop maybe. I'm not sure.

"Let's chill in here so they can't find us."

For the countless time this evening I'm a little confused again. Not sure what's going on. Confusion must be contagious here. Sensing my drunk wonderment...

"They will drag me home. They hate when I talk to guys."

She's done this before.

"I will drag you home. I hate guys do stuff."

This is awesome. Why couldn't the hot girl from home that I had a connection with do this sort of thing? Her stupid friends always dragged her away. Jealousy is an evil bitch, especially when spawned in an evil bitch friend miles away at another house sending a cab over to pick her up. She had to ask for my address three times because I refused to give it up. When I finally did I gave the wrong one - think I sent the cabbie to a shopping mall.

"Let's go to my hotel... they will never find you." in a poorly timed rapist voice.
"Good idea."
"Really? Sweet"

I had her at herpes.

I wake up from a pain coming from inside. Stomach or head, can't figure out which feels worse. They cancel each other so I'm my normal just-below-shitty feeling self. Some girl is next to me, the one from last night I assume. She's not too bad looking, but still not a girl you would smile about while telling your buddies how you got drunk and fucked last night.

Did we?

I'm shirtless but still have my pants and socks on. Usually everything is tossed about, landing on stuff around the room like gum and shaving commercials. Her shirt is still on, completely bottomless though. Never a big fan of the upper body, don't mind it, but total butt guy. I don't have to stretch far to figure out what happened here. I hope I didn't cry or something. Hour long rants about other girls always makes the one next to me so horny. I would be a regular Casanova if that were true. I have enough emotional ammo to hand out endless orgasms to multiple women for many a night in a row. They say I'm unlike anyone they've ever been with - an emotionally, sexy, scarred dynamo. They won't really understand what they are saying but they won't care. If I had to rationalize everything that turns me on, I would be fucked – figuratively, unfortunately.

I hear the shower running.

Time for one anyway.

I run it warm until I get in and slowly push it to scalding. My hands link behind my neck while I sink into my daily, sometimes weekly, time warp of existential thoughtlessness. It's the closest thing to my rain fetish that I can fabricate without a universal studio budget. A bunch of stuff goes through my head. I mouth responses to conversations that I wish over. There are hand gestures that follow. I try to stretch my quad and hit my heel on the faucet. It starts bleeding pretty bad so I get out and wrap one of the weird smaller towels that aren't a real towel or wash cloth around it. I confirm the weird towelage when I wrap the second around my fat gut waist. If I connect it in front, each side would be a mere accent to my junk - nice juxtaposition between the clean white and the evil darkness of my centerpiece. I give up on the wrap and just grab myself with the towel as a buffer as I walk back out to the room area. She's sitting on the bed. She puts pants on. That's pretty stupid. My clothes are next to her, not where they were before. That's pretty weird.

"So I guess you're not staying?"
"Nope gotta go"
"Why?"
"California"
"Someone expecting you?"
"Not really"
"Then why must you leave" she must go to college far away.
"..."
"There's no reason for you to go immediately"

"Yeah but... an afternoon will turn into a night, a night into a couple days, those into weeks, weeks into a long enough time where we want to murder each other."
"Take me with you."

Jesus shit we had to've done it through my pants last night.

"I'm not even close to ready to have another relationship."
"It's not a relationship. I'm just tagging along."
"I know a relationship when I see one and that would be the beginning of such."

She bitches and complains about wanting to come with me and how she's not attached to me or anything - red flag. Already the bitching, complaining and denial?

"Alright.. I'll tell you exactly why this can't work."
"Ok..." shutting me out of her head.
"I tell you from the beginning that I don't want you to come and that none of what we do means anything - no more than face value. We will ride for a while. Everything will be good for a bit, but then you will start talking about plans for when we get there. Plans that I had no plan on thinking about. I will remind you of what I said before. You will get upset and want to jump off the train (car). No matter where you get out, you'll be pissed since you are nowhere close to home. It'll take you a while to get back. The whole time you will hate me, yell stuff about me and blame all your shit on me even though I didn't want you to come in the first place."

She, understandably, gets real pissed and heads for the door without a word. I feel a little bad, but I know if I say it any other way I wouldn't be able to get my point across and I would inevitably allow her to join. Then everything would go according to prediction. Feeling the need to say something, I stop her before she gets out the door.

"Yes...?"
"Did we do it?"

With a look of disgusted confusion as to how I could ask/not know, "Realy?! No. We didn't do it. I said I didn't want to. Then you just bitched about other girls for an hour while I tried to go to sleep."

She slams the doors.

It hurts my ears.

I laugh.

I knew it.

Back on the road, alone, how I like it. I am already lonely. Why couldn't I have let her come for a day or two? Because a day or two snow balls into her far from home hating me. Oh yeah. Can't do that to her just for some variable company where X equals anyone that will try and pretend to listen. I would have gotten bored or annoyed with her quickly. It's hard to convince away the short coming of another when you are in a car with them on a trip across the continent, especially when I'm not taking the shortest way possible. I grab a car-temp beer - one way to get rid of the short-comings. I reach for cigarettes in my pocket but pull out the greeting cards instead. Hungover, I throw them on the passenger seat, find my cigarettes and continue to breathe more smoke than oxygen for a while.

An upbeat rap song comes on. I roll down the windows even though it's cold outside, turn the heat on full blast. My glasses go on even though it's cloudy dark. My head bobs up and down and I think how the world is ahead of me. I feel big, strong and motivated. The world at my fingertips. I can do anything and will once I get to where I'm going, wherever that is. People will follow what I do and want to meet me. I'll be associated with New York some how. Hot women actresses will tell famous hot guy actors that they met me. I won't remember meeting them.

The song ends.

I feel like shit again.

Reminded of how annoying girls are, I pout and stay in the car for the next couple days. Avoid towns. They are all the same anyway so what's the point of stopping? I need variety, not monotony. That's why I'm just driving and sleeping in the car - intellectually stimulating. I am so stupid. The things I do for spite, even when I'm spiting myself, are ridiculous. It's not even spite now, maybe stupidity - always a possibility.

These days are spent in my head playing out countless situations I may or may not ever be subjected to. A lot of cringing on my part. Some goosebumps. Everyone has thought about how great it would be to be a kid again. I'm just like them, except I put some modifications on it; like me not being fat or so big-headed, literally. I don't want such a big head when I go back. Lots of sad things come to mind. I think about what I would do if my parents died. Not my favorite thought. It's going to be great when I'm famous. I can't wait to see for what. Maybe for something legendary. Maybe for something terrible. Doing something terrible is too easy. I won't do anything like that. What if I just drove into the wilderness and never came back... I don't think anyone would care that much. No one would notice for a while. Even when they would they would think I just am away for a while. What if I had sex with a deer and had deer-human children. Only constructive mind-wandering for me. The doe would probably get an abortion anyway. After all, deer/human breeding is forbidden among the deer population.

And it's about time to start meeting people again.

VIII

This place is... I don't even care. Imagine it for yourself. I'll give some hints. There are an ass ton of trees driving in and there are no signs as to where I am. Parking is readily available. The hotel is a hotel the size of a small mansion I would think twice about moving into even if it were free with employees and rooms. The people wear warm shirts and jeans that aren't baggy or tight. It's getting dark. I can already see stars.

Low ceilings and dimly lit, there's no young crowd here. Wonder how is the Puerto Rican crowd. Lot of old dudes, probably hunters. Not looking for them but they are always good for stories. It's a horseshoe bar so everyone can inconspicuously stare at each other. I'm on the side facing the door, a seat like the one back home in the bar down the street, the best seat in town. Usually I would like this, but in a place like this, hopefully you imagined correctly, out-of-towners are looked at like a deer in the crosshairs. It's a little unsettling, but so is picking up and driving cross country without a plan or good direction with only the reason you're running away to think about.

I have the personality to mesh with most. No need to be worried. As long as I don't order something *faggy* I will at the very least be left alone. I stick with my whiskey of choice, Mr. John Jameson, and America's own, but Belgian owned, Bud heavy. It comes in a pounder can, label regular except with some flare from wherever the hell Belgia is...

The crowd is large but quiet now, maybe third shift waiting to head in, maybe second just out, maybe it's Sunday. Who cares. Everyone is keeping to themselves either way - better than hassling me. I'm running low so I order another round. The bartender turns to go get it. The door opens and a man, tall as I am average and a big nose, leans down and walks in.

"Ranger!" from the bartender, annoying to me.
"What up Bot?!" the tall distresser responds.

Bot?

Everyone turns around. The mood in the place lifts immediately. They all welcome one way or another. Some raise a glass just above the bar and mumble gibberish. Others manage a few syllables. No matter the response, all of their brows are heightened after this giant joins us. Definitely from around here, flannel and jeans. Local legend? Seeing that I'm the foreigner here, nobody has sat near me, leaving only seats next to me open. He might need a few. Think I might make my first non-money-driven contact of the evening – I thought the first would be with a woman but that's looking a bit bleak.

The bartender slides my beer and shot to me as the big nosed goliath lumbers over. My accompanying action is a nervous tick of chain-sipping. When I don't know what to do, I put a drink to my face. Sometimes I don't even drink any of it, another method of hiding. I cannot be expected to talk while I'm drinking. I pseudo-sip away as my soon to be bar-neighbor posts up next to me. I think he's staring at me. I tilt my head upward toward him sipping my beer so I'm not expected to talk.

"You're in my seat." loud enough for the whole bar to hear.

Everyone smiles, some laugh too.

Appreciated.

I subdue my nervosa and place my drink two seats down.

"Sorry I didn't know..." face down sliding past him like I'm scaling the side of a mountain with three inches of ledge.

He grabs me. Flashes of the door being locked and everyone unbuckling themselves run through my head. I always knew I was going to die surprisingly. My one stipulation was that it wouldn't involve gang rape. I don't even know why I try to plan things at all. I hope Paul Bunyan goes first so the rest of the gang goes close to unnoticed. He probably will - seems like the town hero. He most likely built the biggest tree fort, caught a whale out the 'crik' and raped the elusive mountain lion among other major accomplishments.

'Ranger' laughs with his mouth half closed. It's more of a repetitive 'huhhuh' rather than 'haha'. It sounds perfect for someone who is about to have his way with me - actually what the girls sound like too.

I take the shot to ease what's about to happen.

"I'm just kiddin' with ya bot! Relax. Sit down." pushing me back to my original seat.
"Oh... Yeah... Thanks."

Thanks? By this time everyone is out loud laughing. I yell "Come on... He's big!" That last shot worked fast. They all appreciate the humility whether or not they know it.

"What swill ya drinkin'"?
"Swill? Oh... Jameson."
"Ahh. Knew it. Get him another... How do you drink that stuff?" gesturing my way to the bartender almost hitting me with his fingers.

Must be like carrying a ladder - forget how long it is and *boom* a child dies.

Still on a high from responding earlier, I'm speechless. He goes on to explain how I'm drinking beaver piss and orders us a 'real drink' - Knob Creek. We toss it back. No better or worse in my opinion considering all liquor makes me look like a chick felating for the first time - little confused, and then a fight against vomiting. Everyone laughs at me again. It's like we are on stage and everyone is eager to see what stupid thing I do next. "Smooth" I say once I swallow and return to normal.

"Good." he says as he orders another round.

I don't think he pays much here.

I realize I haven't introduced myself. Upon doing so he replies "Nice to meet you" and never tells me his name like I'm supposed to know it already. Arrogant but I don't take it that way. Maybe he figures I heard it called when he came in. I did, along with the attention seeking leaches that fill the rest of the bar. Since he came in it has been 'Ranger how bout this', 'Ranger how bout that','Ranger I love you'. He doesn't seem to mind. I would. Every sentence followed by that person looking at me, 'Right...?!' 'Yes. Yes.' I would say patting whoever on the head hoping they leave me alone.

Ranger is a trip. He talks with his limbs, not as much as Italians but since he's so long, it's about the same. He hunts and fishes and claims that he has since he was three years old. I don't doubt it. He was probably taller than me at that age. Shot his first buck at eight. Went on his first solo fishing trip up the mountain when he was four. Loves 80's metal and knows everything about classic rock. When a song comes on that he doesn't prefer, he demands change calling it 'druggie trash' or 'fem-bot pop'. He pumps ten bucks into the jukebox to cut the line at the source. I don't mind. He keeps ordering rounds.

We're at the pool table in the back playing two of the other locals. He has his own stick. I would normally think he's a loser for having one, but it's kept behind the bar. Not sure why that makes a difference but it does. He even lets me use it since we are on the same team. Feeling younger by the minute. He's good. I'm hit or miss, mostly miss. I manage to hit in some easy shots. I can hear him say something like "...ohh ball striker..." laughing about something else at the same time. It's hard to get mad since I'm playing like shit. I'm not in the place or company to get mad at anything. I scratch on my next shot. Ball striker me. The guy on the other team hits a shot or two before Ranger eventually takes over and wins the game on an unnecessary one-handed trick shot.

"Nice shot... Too bad no bitches were around to see that one!" drunk.
"Why? They can't play pool."

I give a smile as if I just told a joke that everyone heard but didn't respond to because it wasn't at all funny. Point taken. I try to cover and explain how I need to get laid.

"Hell... Just walk outside and 20 feet into the woods... You'll get somethin"

Flashes of gay group sex run back through my head. I laugh knowing this isn't the first time today I've thought about getting gang raped. We're all drunk. I want one semi-attractive girl to look at right now and he just keeps reverting back to guy shit. Am I being lured into a false sense of security before they eventually close the bar and have their way with me? Whatever I'll just get super drunk so I won't remember anything. That's a good idea - staying.

Two Knob Creeks please.
Pounders please.
Knobs please.
Beers.
Shots.
Shbeeers.
Snots.
Shmeearbs.
showelits.

The rest of the night flies by like high school. I scratch more and more. I say a lot of sentences including the word *seriously* and *bitches* in regards to where they are. Closest thing to a woman I remember is some guy that had longer hair and real red cheeks. Must be poor blood circulation or rosacea. He's ugly though so no worries there. It's getting about that time where the bar should be closing. God only knows if this place actually ever closes. I imagine the cops don't care. I'm pretty sure there was one throwing his badge on the pool table as a wager earlier. The town's elite chosen by drunken bar games. The way it should be. I should probably get out of here before I over stay my welcome. Of course it's not that easy. It's 4AM.

"Alright! Everyone who is in, is in!" the bartender yells standing by the front door dangling the key between his fingers.

'Oh Jesus shit' I think this so hard I feel like everyone heard me. They just stare at me and laugh like they were before. A bowel-moving panic sweeps deep into my colon. If I was on a toilet I wouldn't have to push so much as just let go. They have been laughing at me the whole time, not because of the stupid funny shit that was happening, but because of what they all knew was going to happen around 4 o'clock. Nothing good ever happens after 4 o'clock. I try casually walking to the door, for some reason slightly waving bye to Ranger.

"Where do you think you're going?" light-hearted for him, terrifying for me. "The night's just starting!"

He pushes me back toward the soul television in the place. The others have been setting up chairs and barstools in a circle around the front of the TV. Ritualistic. Welcome to this town. Another dude sits me down.

"Rookies in front"

I sit down like a sheepish little bitch. No wonder no one really talked about bitches not being around. There was one this whole time.... ME. Everyone is getting settled, me center stage. The lights dim lower than what they were. I feel the eyes of each dude checking me out. The bartender appears next to em, bottle of Knob poking me in the shoulder...

"You start!" with a lick of his lips.

Well, I can thank Christ for this offering to soften the blow((s) to my butt). I guess I'll be riding an invisible donkey to the foot of St. Peter. Lying in bed next to a girl I convinced myself to love doesn't seem like a bad thing right now. Nothing seems like a bad thing at this second. I take an extra swig of the Creek. They probably make me drink this because it's nice foreshadowing for what's to come. My last chug from the bottle is followed by cheers from the crowd. I pass it to my right. Ranger walks to the front and into the circle with a hand behind his back.

I figured.

"Alright everyone shut the hello up!!" as he reveals what's behind him.

To my surprise, it's not an arm-sized dildo, but a video tape. Ok. I guess they need some hot guy porn to get them started. Whatever. By this time I'm all sorts of fucked in every way you can imagine. He plops it in. I close my eyes listening to the intro music. Must be a western porn. Everyone cheers. Must be the opening scene. Not wanting to go out a little bitch, I open my eyes - either way I'm going out a bitch but that's not important - it is, but there's no changing it so whatever.

TOMBSTONE

Tombstone? Everyone continues cheering. Little confused but not wanting to be left out I start cheering along - half for *Tombstone*, half for at least temporarily not getting things shoved up my butt

I know this movie is awesome, but I forget how long it runs. It doesn't really matter. At 4AM a commercial can seem like an eight part mini series narrated by Morgan Freeman. A bottle of Knob Creek circulates during the entire movie. Once one is done, the bartender grabs another one from the back. No one drinks anything else. I don't think we are allowed. We cheer for Doc Holliday, Wyatt Earp and the others (except for Bill Paxton/Pullman's character because he sucks) whenever anything awesome happens. There are some parts they cheer for and I'm not sure why. They have definitely done this before. I cheer anyway. One of those things where you have to watch the movie thousands of times, like me and my friends with The Last Waltz. When Richard Manuel calmly explains the origin of The Band's name sake and ends with an aggressive *THHHEEE BAANDD* we all go nuts and punch each other. Granted it's usually 5AM on the weekend, but then again, what day is it?

The movie is ending. All characters still alive are parting ways. If most of these guys didn't kill things as a hobby, they would probably be crying. The credits roll. Everyone gets up and starts putting the chairs away. As guys stumble out the door they throw bills on the bar, lots of ones and fives. Nothing to cover even close to what was consumed, more of a gesture of thanks between close friends who don't expect anything from each other. It comes around. Karma isn't always a secret evil abortion having bitch. Not ever carrying too much cash I throw all I have. I nod drunkenly to the bartender in more of an effort to not let my head flop off my shoulders.

It's daylight.

Like six or something.

"Alright! Who's fishing?" Ranger yells to everyone still milling about the parking lot.

Fishing? That shouldn't be a question, more of an *ugg... fishing*. At least for me

"I know it's a lil late, but I bet there are still some fish floppin around" Ranger explains to the tweeners.

"Yeah maybe for you!" from a guy that would've been about seventh in line to rape me.

"Huhuh... Come on... I'm your huckleberry... I'll give you five how 'bout?" looking into his own truck assuming no one is going.

No one does.

Except me.

Casually forgetting I don't have a rod or know how to fish, "stop for some coffee and I'll head out with you." Some of the others look at me and chuckle to themselves loud enough for me to notice."

"Good luck guy!" from the one that probably wouldn't've gotten it up because of my baby smooth ass.

"Well check out ball-striker over here..." with an astonished laugh of surprise "You gotta rod?
"Nope." floating down Knob Creek and avoiding embarrassment.
"Know how to fly fish?"
"Nope." not even listening to what Ranger is saying.
"Huhuh... this should be a fun run!" getting into his NRA-stickered F-150 "Hop in!"

I do as I'm told by the leader of the local population in fear of a public display of discipline. Not really, but feared similar things over the last 24 hours. Why stop now. Fishing may be code word for butt rape. Let's hope not... or some shit.

We drive down the road with scenery I'm familiar with over the last however long since I left. Lots of woods and side 'roads' ominously leading off to what appears to be nowhere, or somewhere I just don't want to be. We stop at a convenient store littered with handmade signs for live bait. Inside I find the coffee. While pouring I ask what kinda bait we're getting. Standing a foot above the aisles he stops mid pace and stares at me, mean as what I originally thought everyone would be.

"Huhuh... you better be jokin"
"Yep, totally"
"Real fishermen don't use bait"
"Duh" wondering then what the hell they catch fish with.

Back in the car he's mumbling something about a river running through something when I ask where we are going as if I would be familiar with any place he would say.

"Big Cove."
"Sounds interesting. A lot of people go there?"
"Only the ones that have been there before..."
"But I've never been there before..." confused and wondering if I'll remember this in the late afternoon.

"Huhuh... looks like I'll have to kill ya then."

I laugh believing, hoping he's kidding. The events of the last night/this morning have calmed me down as far as getting killed/raped. We bullshit back and forth. I ask him if he has a rod for me. He seems disgusted. Not from the phallic sounds reference, but rather that I would think that he doesn't have one for me. He's going to have to teach me how to fly fish. He says he doesn't mind and that a buddy of his will be there to help as well. I assume out loud that he's been there before. He laughs and validates my assumption. Apparently I'm going to like this guy.

I take his word

We part from the main road onto one of those side 'roads' made of gravel. Gravel turns into dirt and dirt into straight mud. Branches over hang the 'path', scratching the shit out of the truck. He says that's what trucks are for. There's a dog rustling around in a bush. It looks like the product of generations of slutty mutt breeding, most generic looking dog I've ever seen. Really unappealing. It starts to shit. We both laugh and make comments and laugh some more. We pull up to a clearing next to the *crik*. There's a homemade picnic table, a tent, another pickup and a guy with a case of Bud heavy smiling like he boned someone out of his league. Ranger continues laughing but now at the dude standing there.

"There he is.." exclaiming with even more laughter.

He hasn't really stopped laughing since last night. I can't keep up with it. I would have to watermark over the text with 'huhuh's to show the consistency. It lifts the mood of everything around him, just like hours ago when he first stepped into the bar. I'm used to the opposite, everything sucking the life out of me.

Nice change.

Let's go fishing.

I get out of the car and Ranger's friend looks surprised that there's someone else with him. We are introduced. He's one of the stand-offish types. He has a slight frown like he's about to get raped by a bar full of locals. I know the feeling, but I don't think it's that. He's just shy.

"How's it going?" I ask shaking his hand.
"Fine." looking confused why I'm saying hello, shaking his hand, or both.

Ranger yells something to him. His eyes light up and he starts spewing out random info about the weather - *crik* flow, sun risin', bugs fallin', along with a bunch of other stuff I don't know enough about to care. He's a passionate one - fishing and apparently booze. There is an armful of empty beers in his bed. I hear beers crackin'. Both are staring at me, waiting for me to join in for an assumed pre-fish ritual. I grab one from the case, crack accordingly and let the foam flow to the ground.

"To the fish!"

They both give me a look of *why not?* as I walk over and cheers.

After the beer Ranger starts throwing me his extra everything - rod, waiters, tackle box(don't think they call it that but shut up), license and whatever else. I'm all set to look like I know what I'm doing. I kinda need to pee but I'm not about to hold up the rest of the process. I'll pee myself before I hold them from their fishing. I can only imagine I've already been a bother. They haven't killed me yet and that's a good thing.

"Ok. What do you want to do?" Ranger asks staring off somewhere.
"I'anno" the friend replies. I think it was 'I don't know', but I can't be sure.
"Alright... Take him up stream and fish down. I'll go down and we will meet back here."

What? Mr. grumbles a lot? I want to learn how to fish though. That's kinda a lie. I just want to hang out and drink through my inevitably oncoming hang over. Ranger walks off downstream. Before he steps two steps out of sight I remind him he doesn't have any beer with him.

"Ah I'm good thanks. There's fish to be had!" skipping over trees along the way.

Jesus. He must really love fishing. Fishing for me is up there with golf, bowling, basketball and just about any other activity I do - I do it just to drink with friends. My new partner sees my dumbfoundation and informs me that Ranger doesn't have time to drink beers because he catches too many trout. I think it may be the opposite for me. This is going to be interesting. Not just the fishing, but my silent co-fisher as well. I look at him, at the beer and back at him.

"Wanna finish the case before we hit the *crik*?" I ask with extended pauses between words.
"Yes." he answers with a necessary emphatic head nod.
"Should we shotgun a couple before we head out?" more saying we are going to than asking.
"Yes. Yes we should." his head almost falling off his shoulders.

We shotgun beers and the tension slips away like the excess beer down through the hairs of my ever mounting fire-red beard that I haven't noticed growing. He wins. I don't care for many reasons. My dad has always reminded me that I chug like my mother. She isn't good. Thinking about it now, there might be some sexual undertones to that. Gross.

We are both satisfied enough for the time being to start our little mini-journey. We agree to finish the majority of the beer before we start fishing. Some rules are implemented. For every fish caught, the other shotguns a beer. For every fish not caught, both shotgun beers. There are some more. All include forcing someone, if not both, to be drinking at all times. I think I made a new friend

The hike isn't too too bad. Some fallen trees have to be scaled, but other than that the only hang up is getting my rod caught in things. No fun. He knows the trail well. You would think I know it just as well. It parallels the *crik*. We exchange drunk stories from past endeavors. We share what we thought of each other at first glance. He thought I looked like a douche (and must still since I haven't changed, but whatever). I tell him I just assumed he was illiterate and admit that I kinda still do. We both laugh like assholes as we start cheers-ing to everything.

After what seems like some time, we get to the starting point. We both have to piss and do so a foot off the path. We sit a foot off our pee ponds and have another beer before we dive in. I think both of our fishing expectations are down. He probably won't catch much fish and I most likely won't even throw a line in the water. I think we are set.

It's like I'm five all over again. He sets up all this shit that, not being a fly fisherman, I had no idea about. I thought it was just a line and a hook. The hook having a bunch of shit on it to make it look like a bug or an egg or whatever the hell fish eat. There's like five different sections of line on this thing, each one smaller and more impossible to see than the last. He gets everything all set for me and shows me how to cast. I tell him "I don't get it" as I open another beer. Pretty drunk by this time, "Fuck it." He laughs and casts mine like you're supposed to for me. He does everything but catch the fish for me. He's a few feet downstream from me explaining how to pull this back while pushing that this way and something else, all while he is doing it himself. He is fishing.

"Just use mine" nosing to his rod laying on the bank.

I do my best to mimic what I think he just did. The thing goes plop and I'm now fishing. My legs are tired from the mild hike, mostly from carrying all those beers. He's down stream about 20 feet. I sit down in front of a comfy looking rock, continue to drink my beer and play fly swatter with my rod - so he would think I'm trying. He took his beer sac off and left it next to me. I'm set.

He eventually turns around and asks if I need anything. I can tell he doesn't really care because he B-lines right for the beer.

"Think I'm alright here bud.. You can toss me another though while you're up."

Grabbing me one he finally notices I'm just sprawled out on the bank now.

"Yeah fuck this." in a condoning tone, throwing, not tossing me the beer as he sits back himself. We both crack them open like it was choreographed. We cheers to *fucking this shit* like assholes and swig back our Belgians. Two similar people can be huge motivational influences on each other, for bad, or even worse in this case. He and I seem like two of (in?) the same. One of those things you know right away, after of course the one stops thinking the other's illiterate and vice versa except a douche. We feed off each other's energy/drunk exponentially until a max is hit, most likely a black/pass out. If we met in an intelligent atmosphere, we would probably bring home the Pulitzer. We met at a camp accompanied by a case of beer. I don't think they give Pulitzers for pissing. I could be wrong though. I don't know.

We sit as far apart as we were fishing, legs spread like bored children forced to go outside and play on a nice day sitting in the yard in plain view of the kitchen to show their parents exactly how terrible what they are doing to them is. We want to be here though. We are drunk enough to start having man talk. He asks if I 'gotta girl'. I give the *hmmmph*-laugh and breath out a no, not feeling like going into it. He may or may not sense that and replies with a similar chuckle and a 'me neither'. Aspirations become a popular subject - picture perfect coming from two half-wit fisherman that got too drunk on the way to even fish. *All I need to do is... I'm the type to... With just a little money...*

We aren't going to do shit... Ever. Besides maybe pass out. We pass out without rods in our hands, accomplishing nothing.

I wake up however long later to a laugh that sounds like it's coming from the mountain tops. I have no idea where I am and am still visibly drunk on my back from whatever I was doing before I passed out. Ranger splits the tree line and starts laughing the *huhuh*s again at both of our dead looking bodies on the bank. Last thing I remember is the pre-emptive babble that usually precedes some bro hugs. My partner in drunk-bank-laying is still passed out. Ranger keeps calling us names I assume are insulting. I'm not paying too much attention. My focus is on getting back in my head as well as not throwing up on myself. There's no headache, but laying in the sun in chest high waiters is a nice combo for some sort of bodily function. It's coming out eventually.

"Huhuh... look's like ya got somethin there bot." raining down from the heavens, exaggerated by me laying on the ground.

There's a wiggle in my hand. My senses are coming back. It's not me in my hand. This time it's a fly rod. That's different. I can tell it's a rod by my visual cues - looking and seeing there's a fishing rod down there - along with feeling cues - my junk swimming in a slosh of ass-sweat-soaked boxers instead of my clammy right hand. I sit up and reel in the line.

"Bahhh HAHAH! I caught something!"

Ranger laughs and congratulates me on my first fish. I throw a rock dangerously close to the other's passed out face to wake him up. His eyes half open he mutters out a 'huh'? I lift the fish out of the water. It's a bass. It's supposed to be a trout. It's not a good thing but I take it as such anyway. He's not getting up so I take my *crik* bass and rub it on his face. Opening his eyes to full capacity he realizes that it's not that semi-attractive slut he picked up at the bar one time. He jumps.

"What the fu...?!?! Get that out of my face!"
"Look! I caught a fish!" batting it at his face until he finally gets up and runs into the brush up the bank. "Just wanted to show you my fish!"
"Fuck your fish. It's a bass it doesn't count. They are stupid."
"Hey... HEY!..."
"What?!"
"Where's your fish?"
"I don't have one."
"So Mr. Big-Fisher-Guy doesn't have a fish and I do?!"
"Shut up."
"Even caught it sleeping!"
"Shut up."
"I believe that means I'm a better fisherman than you."

We jabber back and forth for some time. He gets borderline seriously angry, but realizes how silly it is right before he does. I ask Ranger how many he caught hoping it was zero so I can be the greatest drunk sleeping fisherman ever. He says he lost count half way to here. I would normally be skeptical of this because I'm always skeptical and pretty much don't believe anyone, but seeing that he has already caught three while we were jibber-jabberin' back and forth, I'm inclined to believe him.

Already hung over and still exhausted from the hike, forgetting even about last night, we decide to pass out at the camp. Not Ranger though. He says there's still fish to be had. Ranger heads up stream as we head back to camp.

I find an attractive spot in Ranger's truck. Thank Ford for their bench seating. Face down toward the NRA floor mats I start to fall in and out of a dream. I start twitching like I'm sleeping next to someone new. So drunk and tired, this doesn't last as long as it usually does. I drift off.

I wake up and I can't remember my dreams. My head is partially lodged face first in the seat crack in the front of Ranger's truck - would be the whole way if it were at all physically possible. I pull my head out while my forehead skin slowly molds back to my face. I may have pissed myself. At least it's not shit. I feel like it though. Cannot tell if the sun is coming or going. No idea where is East or West. Let's hope it is going because waking up in the morning with this kind of hangover is just balls and nuts to the face. I sit up rubbing my face like there is another one underneath.

Bah.

Good to go.

My new friend hears me get out of the truck. He is scurrying around the fire pit looking like he is attempting to try and start something. We look at each other and both laugh at how ugly the other is. I yell '*bahh!*' and head for the cooler. I ask if he wants one and he looks at me like there is no way.

"What? I thought you were some country boys."
"I'm good."
"No you're not." throwing, not tossing, a beer directly at his face "ya pussy."

I have never liked that word, but it fits so well right now. With a deep sigh and possible mini-throw-up his head falls in submission and cracks the shit open. We cheers like tired assholes, swig and start getting the fire going - for actual now. A mound of sticks and a couple trees worth of logs and the fire is above our heads, undoubtedly killing the branches above. Everything dies some time.

"When do you think Ranger will get back?"
"He'll fish till it's pitch... Then realize he's an hour walk away. Hard to say."
"Jesus."

We sit around the fire about ten feet off. Buzzes return quickly during our little bender. Out in the woods it is an unspoken point to get as blasted drunk as possible. History has hilarious reasons for doing so - lots of nudity and near-death-experiences. I ask him if he wants to play a game. He is reluctant. I explain that there's no homo shit involved. He's still not budging. He's comfy in the half sleeping state he's been fighting for the last hour. He finally gasps and tells me we do not have any cards.

"Good! We don't need any!"
"Ummm... Ok..? What's the game?"
"Big Fat Hen."

He looks confused. Rightfully so. No one ever knows this game when I bring it up unless I've already played it around them. I still have one friend that holds me personally responsible for a huge scar he suffered during the tail end of a round - got so drunk he tripped into a pool, gashing his leg from one side to the other on the concrete edge. Still contacts me from time to time to remind him how to play the game.

"What the fuck is 'Big Fat Hen'?"
"It's easy. You just have to repeat after me."
"That's not good."
"There are a few rules too."
"Oh shit."

RULES of BIG FAT HEN: Every mistake is one drink[1]

1.) Repeat after me.

2.) No pointing with anything below the elbows[2] by anyone

3.) No cursing[3] by anyone

4.) No help from the audience[4]

A recommendation is to pick someone already kinda hammered. Memory games are a bunch more difficult/fun when drunk.

---

[1] One Drink = (men) 1 shot, (boys) 1/3 of beer, (females) they cheat anyway so it doesn't matter
[2] *Below the Elbows* is defined according to the anatomical position - arms straight down to the sides
[3] *Cursing* is anything you wouldn't say to your grandmother (if you say whatever to your grandmother, cursing will be acknowledged at my discretion.)
[4] The audience is always inclined to help from their own drunken stupor. This ruins the game. If they attest that they can do whatever they want, challenge them to play. They will say no. No one will like these people.

He looks confused, but not wanting to listen to the rules again he says he is ready. I tell him to drink a beer while I go piss. Actually, I'm just making sure I remember the whole thing. It's a set of ten phrases. My dad learned it on a bottle of George Dickle. I learned it from him on a camping trip once. He was actually playing with someone else, but I tell everyone I learned it on George Dickle too. Shhhh. The funny part of this game is that the subject always thinks it goes back and forth. The expression on their faces when they find out it's just me with the phrases is a mix of *oh shit* and *oh fuck*. Mine... *oh yesssssss.*

"Ready?" strutting in from pissing
"Yeah..." hopelessly.
"Ok."
"Ok."
"No not yet."
"No not yet."
"Shut up it's a set of 10 phrases!"
"Oh."
"Ok" with a deep breath "Big fat hen."
"Big fat hen."
"Big fat hen. Couple ducks."
"Big fat hen. A couple duck."
"Nope!"
"The fuck?!"
"Drink again!"
"Shit!"
"And again." pointing to his drink with my elbow.

We are at a loss for booze so it's beer for him. Three thirds to be specific. He chugs like a drunk and we begin again.

"Ok my turn." he says with assurance.
"Nope. That's not the game."
"What the fuck?"
"You have to repeat after *me*... and drink please."

He's out and walking to the cooler for another beer most likely thinking something between *fun* and *awful*. Should get a few it'd probably save some time. He may be pissing himself already. He asks what he got wrong. A stickler for the rules I tell him I can't tell him and repeat rule #4. He voice-vomits a loud '*BAHH!*' and we continue as he calls me an asshole, pointing at me with his pointer finger. I wait for him to drink another beer and then ask where the cooler is. I wait again for him to drink for pointing at the cooler and swearing.

This goes on for a bit. He slowly curbs his language. The pointing thing isn't too bad for him, except when I ask where things are. People say the game is unfair because I never have to drink. They are mistaken. Whenever I mess up I have to drink as well, plus I eventually get somewhere close to bored and start aggressively casually drinking while paying attention once every moment or five. This goes on for a couple more bits more. He's getting high school drunk and his responses are getting more and more ridiculous. In mid laugh I hear a voice behind me and nearly jump into the fire to escape.

"Ranger!"
"Hey kids. What's happenin?!" splitting the outlining tree tops.
"Big fat fucking hen is going on..." I hear over my shoulder near the cooler radiating from not the air but the ground that he's now using as a temporary bed.
"Drink" pointing at him with my elbow - after playing this game you end up pointing at things with your elbow for a couple months. I haven't pointed with anything below my elbows in years.
"Looks like I have some catch up to do" Ranger says stepping over our friend on the way to the cooler.

I explain the rules again and continue to get completely camping drunk. Ranger finds the game hilarious. The phrases are getting more and more absurd. He is at nine now, no small feat.

"Nine nerdy nymphos knockin knock knock on a heaven's door and Axel is an asshole!"
"Almost... drink." as I laugh along with Ranger, handing him a beer for his faults. "Think it's time for a break."
"Thank Christ" our evening entertainment exclaims as he goes to shit, piss or pass out. Not sure which exactly. He's gone for a little. Neither of the rest of us notice.

Not as drunk as my big fat hen, I'm a little hammered. Ranger is catching up quick, rehydrating with a quick seven beers. Beer for water always does magic on your system. I've been a little slow on the re-ups. Between that and Ranger slugging, it seems we have reached a drunk medium.

We chill, poking the fire with deep breaths of *ahhh - life isn't so bad.* Silences always scares me, especially when it's just me and someone else. I have always suspected that I have social anxiety. I've always been marked as an extrovert. I've read some things about introverts. I think I'm that. It's not too bad now. It's been a long day so I don't assume Ranger is thinking about how much of a douche I am like I normally would. I'm trying to think of something to say to break the possibly awkward silence.

"Soo... Gotta girl or somethin'?"

He laughs like it is an off the wall question going on to explain how he doesn't need some she-critter holding him from his life of lux.

Apparently many have tried, none successful. This proud, god-like figure of these whatever mountains can't be held back. It was a ridiculous question. He's probably takes frequent sacrifices in exchange for peace for the town's folk.

Is he just slayin' bitches then?

He laughs like it is a ridiculous question, not sure for a negative or not. I ask if that is a laugh of 'of course' or a laugh of 'are you crazy?!'. Then a slow realization dawns on me that he may be gay.

"You gay?"
"No way... Does it look like I suck cock?" laughing, not insulted.
"Um... Don't think so... I wouldn't give a shit" in contemplative remission

We hear a rustle in the bushes and get up with a flaming poker... from the fire. I yell to see if someone is there.

"Bahhh! I'm the ghost of Drunkard's past!!"

It's Big Fat Hen, most likely lost on his way back to the fire.

"You lost?"
"No... Just came back the wrong way."
"Oh ok... What were you doing?"
"Bud Mud."

Knowing the trials of Bud Mud I nod my head - never leaves you until you stop drinking for a couple weeks. Usually hits at the worst times. He sits tenderly in his spot and kinda passes out, but not the whole way, or something.

"Let me tell you thing..." Ranger inviting me back from my bud mud nightmare.
"OK." with thoughts of some sort of religious cult talk coming my way.

Fears from before of public sodomy and bestiality mudslide up from my stomach. Besides the lack of audience I feel not so good right now.

"I'm the founder of the Penguin Club."
"Fuck is the Penguin Club?!" I drink (broke rule #3).
"Huhuh... You never heard of the Penguin Club?!" Good Lord!"

So he does it with Penguins? Where the shit does he find penguins around here? Maybe his pull runs deeper than I thought, deep into America's infrastructure. Deep enough to get Penguins on demand. It's really blowing my mind. I don't know if I want to know. Of course I do, I'm camp drunk about now. Plus he made it sound like I'm stupid dumb for not knowing what the hell it is. Big Fat Hen rolls his eyes, half from the Penguin Club mention and probably half from the booze. Laughing at him I let Ranger continue.

> The *Penguin Club:*
>
> One of strength and control. Many try, most follow short. Weak-minded individuals falter under the pressure. Some guise their inabilities as the virtues, but at the end of the year they cannot punch a card. Others bear false truths in attempts to join despite their primal shortcomings. Some make up their own rules because of their situations. True members acknowledge life and take command of their being.

He goes through this speech, much longer than I depict - can only pay attention so long at whatever hour it is being as however drunk I am right now - laughing throughout. Taking in what I remember I sit like a pre-teen taken to a born-again-Christian mass/worship/brunch (or whatever the hell they call it) after being told *I'll be different afterward* wondering to myself afterward when the next opportunity to fornicate will be.

Confused what just happened.

"You can have your Penguin Club Ranger!"
"So what is it exactly? I missed/didn't understand what you were saying."

Ranger *huhuh*s and continues...

"You can only have sex once a year... No more. No less."

He then went on to explain that it's called the penguin club because penguins only mate once a year. He continued to talk while I imagined what it would be like only having sex once a year for forever. I interrupted him mid-sentence:

"I prefer the rabbit club Ranger! The rabbit club!!"

"You'll stick it in anyone. You're out of the club. Not that you were ever in it."

I keep sitting and start laughing out of astonishment, both at Ranger and Big Fat Hen. Well, maybe just Ranger. The rabbit idea sounds more fun to me and did cross my mind immediately upon definition of the Penguin Club. The idea of fucking as many women as possible sounds a lot more entertaining than one a year. There are some points to it though. I ask if it's religious related. Being a semi-strict Catholic he laughs saying that if it was it would be zero until marriage. Should've known. Thirteen years of Catholic school served me well.

The indirect purpose and made up message I find in this whole schpeel is that women are a distraction. They hold us back from what we want to do. But this is confusing because a majority of my time until recently has been spent trying to hump one of them. There's a time and place, like when you get one pregnant. Actually, no. Happened to me and it was an amazing emotional inconvenience. I tricked myself to think it was good only to have it blow up in my face. Inconvenient x2. Maybe it's one of those *wait for the right one* things. You fuck enough people you will eventually convince yourself one of them is right for you, but really not at all when it's done and over - a big screening process for something that doesn't completely annoy you. Dunno. I'm hammered and this guy is talking about having sex once a year. Maybe he has the sex drive of a fish... in that he prefers fish to women.

"Come on... Let's go" Ranger interrupting my day/night dream.
"Where we headed?"
"It's time."

Big Fat Hen gets his big fat ass up and is all excited for some reason. I'm confused per usual as my fears of the mountain sex life sober me up a bit. Used to it now, my caution leaves with another beer. I'm still confused about where we're going. I go anyway - Ranger is convincing like God. He talks in facts, or makes things seem like so - everything necessary and absolute. We go off into the woods. Big Fat Hen is hopping back and forth on the trail like we're headed to a slew of drunk chicks. I watch and laugh and wonder about the events that've lead up to this moment.

"It's been 10 years since we buried it out here."

Turning to the hen who just bounced beside me I ask what the hell Ranger's talking about. Burying something out in the woods sounds a little off and mass-murderish... I'm informed that it's nothing like that and that he himself wasn't there when it was done. Nice. decriminalizing himself. Makes me feel about the same as before.

I light up a cigarette because I want one.

Like the movies I continue to blindly follow them into the middle of the unfamiliar woods. I made a mental note to note how we got out here and then failed to pay attention what the original note was about while thinking about how much taller Ranger is than me.

Guessing about a half hour has passed and he stops.

"We are here." pointing at a tree with the initials K.C. and the year ten years ago.

> Here lays Kelly Christian... A God-fearing virgin sacrificed to the fish gods some ten years ago. She would've been raped but all attendees already had their Penguin Club cards punched for the year (it was late December)

Ranger pulls a shovel out of his ass. Never noticed it was there.

The hole is not big at first, but then again no hole is big at first though. I'm still in the dark in all ways possible. The hole is about a square foot and ranger starts going for depth. A few moments later he strikes something.

Oh good.

A dead baby grave.

"Got it." with a half smile teetering on full.

Things running through my mind that it could be:
Dead baby (obviously)
The head of someone who had sex twice in a year
Some sort of placenta
Penis
More beers

He kneels down hovering over the hole like a virgin puzzled at a vagina. Except he's not confused, just happy. Pulling out a cooler he chuckles like a kid with a present of which he already knows the contents. Ground storages seems safe and sterile, it's definitely an organ or two. He pops off the lid. It's the kind that comes completely off.

Never needing an invite for anything, I peek in without a prompt. Liquid somewhere between piss and runny diarrhea pours out of the cooler revealing a foggy ziplock bag. Remnants of the first hymen of the Penguin Club I now assume. Big Fat Hen is double dutching without jump ropes and squealing. Ranger picks up the bag and opens it. Another cloudy ziplock. If I'm dreaming I'm going to be so pissed.

"Here it is!"
"Finally!"

Ranger holds up the contents. It's a bottle of Knob Creek, surprisingly well-kept in the double ziplock cooler buried at the foot of a tree. Good. We were running out back at camp. I should've seen this coming. Maybe the murky water is some poor girl's something-or-other. Ready to go back.

"Ok. That's neat. What's going on?"
"What?" ranger with a completed grin
"Why are we digging up booze in the middle of the night/woods?"
"It's been ten years."

It's been ten years every day since I turned ten.

A sense of irregularity sets into my chest. Something is sentimental here. My drunk head is putting together some pieces - more so found an already completed puzzle glued together and framed on the wall above someone's unexpected kid they had a couple years ago.

I shut up wondering what the puzzle looks like.

Ranger peels off the original sealing and pops the cork. Swigs are coming, though right now isn't the greatest time for me. Almost sick-drunk already, the fictitious girl's pissy diarrhea seems more appealing than my looming shot. Can't be lame now. Something heart felt and worth remember is coming and I can't deal with that kinda shit with words or experiences. That's a good thing, for me anyway.

Ranger pours a little out next to the tree *to lost loved ones*. Guess that's more than a rap thing. Big Fat Hen's big fat head nods in agreement. Both take a nip and then it's my turn. Holding the bottle in the air I cheers *to good friends*, take a breath and take it to the face. It gets trapped between my lips and reluctant throat. It gets down, painfully and I pass back to Ranger. He takes it like the man he is and starts leading us back. I think of the lack of possibility of me finding a spot like that at any moment in my life. The bottle comes back to me. Oh nice. We are still doing this. I'm a bitch and pretend to drink it whenever it comes around to me.

At the fire. They speak little and me even less. The fire has shrunk a good bit. No idea how long we were gone. We sit in our seats from before. Everyone still silent, I start getting an awkward sweat. Realizing it's hard for me to deal with silence among people, it dawns on me for the first time that I have social anxiety. In addition to this I'm pretty sure that bottle is a monument to a dead friend. Death is not a topic that I can help with at all. Never know what to say in these situations. Seeing that the bottle is almost done and I barely account for three shots, they may just be really hammered. Either way, I usually am the one to help forget. On that note...

"So about the Penguin Club..."

They wobble their heads my way.

"... I'm in."

I end up spending the next couple days with them, remembering after the second that I am still checked into the hotel. I expected to spend the money on lodging anyway so it's not a big issue. It also helps that everything we do is free (except our consistent purchase of any non-light beer). Ranger lets me crash on his couch, but there is little sleeping for anyone. He's some sort of machine. We fish a bunch, shoot some guns until I declare myself a womanly pre-teen who complains about how much her shoulder hurts from the kick of the 12-gauge. I always did get comments on my feminine physique, my fat, feminine physique. Bars are a common coming too, the tab never more than what you would throw at a stripper before you are drunk. No one seems to work, but since I'm no one to comment, I don't. It would suck if they had to, anyway. We are like best friends that grew up together since birth that everyone secretly thinks are gay with each other. We aren't, just to make clear.

I have fun. I forget about the shit that brought me here and stop being a depressed little bitch. I laugh like your cousin you don't like because of that exact thing. It's good. I should stay, but there's nothing here for me. They are hilarious and fun, but I can't stay for anyone besides myself. I catch more fish passed out drunk for the love of hell. I can always meet more people like them. It's always better to end things before they turn to shit anyway. Wouldn't mind meeting up with them down the road. So, hey ho, it's time to go.

"Have fun in California man."
"Thanks. You should come visit."
"Where exactly are you going?"
"Not sure."

Laughing he writes down his address. "I'll give you a head start... Maybe I can catch up once I get tired of this place." giving me the scrap of paper with his chicken shit scratch on it. I take it, smile and nod.

"Alright bot! I'll see ya when I see ya."
"When else would ya?"

Everyone laughs at the small talk that isn't funny. I wave backing out the door of the bar to everyone that cares, or even doesn't, and speed walk to my car. I haven't seen it in days. It's covered in mountain dust and riddled with bird shit.

IX

Thinking back on the past week or so makes me laugh. If someone could see me, they would laugh at me laughing. I laugh at myself laughing. The Penguin Club? The thought of it continues the humor. It would be interesting if I could do it. Pretty much swore off girls anyway. Might as well put a label on it. I think of the last girl I was with and laugh. I find a cigarette. It's sunny and nice, warranting unwarranted laughter and good feelings. I light the cigarette and laugh at how good I feel. Not used to this feeling. It tickles.

It was nice to be social for a bit. That constant isolation was taking a toll. Pessimism breeds on itself like mold. You can't see it right away because it's locked in Tupperware in the fridge. It's there though. It's in the feelings, the sentiments you have for most things. Then one day it's clean-this-disgusting-fridge day and you find what looks like a dead hamster, wondering how this could've ever happened. Miserable. Sad and most likely fat. Actually, maybe not fat since you aren't eating your leftovers.

The drive is nice. My almost finished cig is excellent. My lurking diarrhea is reassuring as well. A trucker passes me and winks. I laugh and speed away from him. I'm not that liberated yet.

There is a calm around me. A relieving calm like when my mom would hug me when I was sad, telling me everything was ok even though it didn't seem like it. I have always assumed they were lying to me, like when they used to explain why their bedroom door was periodically locked. Everything is going to be ok. How or why, I have no clue.

I forget where I am. I have not checked my driving in a while. Looking for a directional sign I speed up. My nerves follow suit with the speedometer, knowing that I'm probably speeding the wrong direction. Since the beginning I've just been going West, following the more interesting numbers. When time and money lose their importance nothing really matters anymore. Especially when you don't want to be around anyone.

Of course, once the money's tight again I'll be finding the most direct road to California.

Ever think about all your friends and wonder what the hell is wrong with yourself?

I see a sign. Says South but the big green ones over the road have roads with West. Can't complain about that. I pick up on the one with the most sexual meaning. Ahh. Sex. Ahh exit ramp 3 lanes over. I quickly and almost without notice cross over all of them nearly killing some people and a dog I locked eyes with. My Jeep skins the right side of the fork off into a westward direction. I'm laughing at what that dog may be thinking. Probably the same as me.

I need to shit.

I drive the rest of the day and into the next. There are enough empty coffee cups in my car to service a small coffee shop with a high ceiling that sells assorted pastries made locally. My diet has been coffee, cigarettes and any music with a good drummer. I start following signs for bigger cities instead of the general West direction. I can't remember if I tried doing this or if I thought I was dreaming. Either way it does not matter since it's the agenda now. Fifty miles to the next big city. I would tell you which, but you would question my timescales and general knowledge of geography.

The city line scape thing is coming into view. It's nice, much better than driving into a town just to realize you are already out the other side. There will be interesting people I don't want to meet here. A lot of hustle and bustle for no reason except for some drive, motivation, willingness-to-succeed sorta bullshit. I'll wonder why I'm there. Then I'll remember *what the hell else should I be doing*. I know a few in this place. Might be another city. I'm not sure. I get them all mixed up, cities and people, since I'm not in or with either, respectively.

The big buildings are around me now. I realize that I, along with all my stupid emotional problems, am small and sit in between an insignificant non-existence. It feels like I could leave my car in the middle of the street and forget about it forever. Could, but won't. You ever feel bad just go to the center of the biggest city near you, look up and know not a soul gives a shit about you or anything about you. You will then feel better. May not work in Iowa.

I wonder what is wrong with me.

I drive around for an hour or two. I'm not sure. Went through a pack of cigarettes I do know though. I settle on a garage that has long term parking for the cost of a year long permit back home. On foot I navigate my way out of the garage for another 15 minutes. Finally free, I stop to get my bearings. Remembering I have none, I start walking.

A few blocks and a bunch of homeless people later I duck into a hotel that probably houses more people than the last however many places I've been in the last whatever. It looks like it would have computers for the customers in the lobby. Hopefully they sell cigarettes so you don't have to steal this service. No cigarettes. Well, I'll be quick. I look up some friends in the area and I'm on my way.

Subway is out. There's just no way I'll ever get it right. Not going to walk for pretty much every reason you can imagine. Let's see if I can do the flaggy thing. It's easy - look like a tourist. I read the address off the back of the hotel card. He doesn't understand me. It should be because of the ethnicity difference, but truth to shit it's because I don't know how to say addresses correctly and I'm about to get fucked on this cab ride. I repeat. He corrects me on how to say it. He doesn't have to ask. I'm not from here. I sit back with my feet on the roof hoping it's quick.

On the ride I play typical tourist, gazing up at everything with my face smashed into the window like it tastes of peanut butter. The window could be rolled down but I've been called a dog one too many times in my life. Having been in the foot hills of bumblefuck for so long it feels like I've been more driving a spaceship than my shitty car. No wonder people want to come here. There's more in a block than my entire home town.

There's no way to know how close we are. The meter is just under absurd now. Not much longer, or maybe. I just want to get there, little anxious. Don't even know what day it is. I nod to some homeless people. Might be homeless one day. Always good to make connections. The cab comes to an abrupt stop. I cough. Dude repeats the address. Time to get out I assume. He says the amount with no reaction from me. No satisfaction for him. I throw my money at him like his mother's a bitch. Standing up I turn around to see what's going on.

We are on the right street and there's a matching number on one of the doors.

The door is up a few stairs. I stand at the first wondering if I should go in, unannounced and all. I'd be lying if I told you this was a random coincidence that she happens to live in the one real city I've stopped in. It is fantastic that I actually got here on purpose somehow.

We went to college together with the same major. She was (and still is) hot so I always asked for study help. I learned later that that's an actual way to get a girl to like you - get her to help you enough until she subconsciously says to herself 'you must like this stupid asshole'. She always had her boyfriend so it was pretty much assumed to be understood to be nothing. Didn't stop me from laying some ground work for a time soon to come. We became friends and like any other pathetic guy with an attractive female friend that talks to him like a person, I fell in love with her, got drunk and told her. She said I didn't. I was confused and repeated myself. You see, because of her boyfriend there was no physical aspect to the relationship, leaving only a mental connection. Unaware that things could work like that, it was different for me. I was troubled how I could feel that way. We never smashed. Thought it was special. I still think there was something there for her, but it was one of those we've-been-together-so-long things. Of course I was (am) a stubborn asshole and could never believe someone wasn't in love with me. I struck too late - end of senior year after she was with what's-his-face for the better duration of academia. Why leave seeming stability for a secret crush you can convince yourself otherwise about. Plus I was having sex with her best friend the whole way through school - another secret of mine.

I'm at the door now, couldn't tell you how I got here if you asked. Still debating on if I should knock or not. I tap the door to a triplet groove. My gut giggles at me while I wait - nothing says hello like runny diarrhea. *No one home* in a half wish. Slowly turning around I start to look for a way out. Anyone ever tells you your terrible sense of awareness is a fault, kick them in the face. We have better things to think about. Reaching for some cigarettes her door now opens to a stop at the end of a security chain.

"Hello?" a little girls voice.
"Hi." without turning around.
"What do you want?" now irritated and annoyed. I can tell - I loved her.
"Can you sit on my face please." turning around hoping the years haven't skewed her voice in my head.
"Oh fuck you."
"It's good to see you."
"You asshooollleeee." as she yells familiarly, tackling me to the ground.

The hallway is small so I hit my head. I squeeze out 'you bitch' as she continues to punch me in the stomach. She's athletic. A girl you playfully wrestle with but secretly try your best so she doesn't embarrass you in front of anyone - she used to kick the shit out of my roommate every weekend.

It's been years, since college to be exact. We hug. I close my eyes like I'm acting. She squeezes harder than me. I don't want to hurt her. She's probably trying. She sits up cowgirl like and slaps me on the chest.

"What's up?!... Come in!"
"Sounds good."

She gets off me and goes inside. I lay there staring at her ass as she walks in. Still makes me tingle. Should be fun.

Her place is a closet of an apartment, not that I care. I would be fine with her living in a box, it's nice to see her. I wouldn't want her living in a box but you know what I mean. She's hustling around trying to find me something to eat or drink. I tell her I'm fine and to sit down so we can chat. She's one of the few that I don't skip beats with. Besides the catching up, it's like we never parted after college - the subtle flirting, innuendoes of being together and the resultant questioning laughter. Catching up is easy when neither of us have much to share. Well, I do have a lot to share, but it can be summed up in a few sentences. We are sitting on a couch facing each other. She looks beautiful, not too much of a surprise.

"So what's up with you?! Way to give me a heads up on you coming here!" she practically yells, knees pointed toward me with her hands on mine.
"Nothing much. Just driving through to Cali." looking down, underplaying the state of my life right now. "Didn't realize I was coming through until I got here."
"Bullshit. You came straight for me." matter-of-factly.
"Haha... Well I knew you were thinking about me..." that bitch.

I believe in both statements. One may be believable than the other. Straight for her might be an extreme, especially since I can't go straight toward any position on purpose (the sentiment probably correct). I've always had the feeling she thinks about me more often than my average friend. I never know what to do about it. She's always here and I've always been where I was. I'm here now with next to nothing to lose. Now's the time, better than any other that I've had, but where's her boyfriend?

"Where's what's-his-face?"
"Oh... he's at work."
"Work? What day is it?"
"Wednesday! You're still a mess!"
"Haha... it's been a bit since I needed to know... Why aren't you at work?"
"Layed off... looking for a job, but I'm good for a couple months."
"Convenient. Buy you a drink?"
"Yes!" with a look from behind bars.
"Let's go then..." trying to hide a smile which makes it even worse.

She takes me to a pub down a couple blocks. I don't care much for the scenery anymore. We talk about the boring stuff from the last couple years since school together - a lot of things that could be better or worse. We laugh at our situations. She can't believe I'm just driving across country by myself. I can't believe she's still with her boyfriend – can, but pissed. I didn't tell her about that. I can totally believe it. I would be surprised otherwise. She'll believe my thing once I get a drink or seven in me and blurt out what happened, thrown in amongst casual conversation. The pub is called 'The Pub'. That's stupid. It's filled with nooks. We sit at the end of the bar against the wall, sequestered from the couple day drunkards and unemployed. The stools are unnecessarily close, neither adjusts when we sit. Two beers, two shots and the two of us.

This should be fun…

"So what's your woman situation like now?"

I laugh, surprised this wasn't the first thing she asked when she was on top of me at her door. She asks again.

"Seriously! Still womanizing everyone you see?"
"Womanizing?" Laughing, never thinking of myself as a womanizer
"Well… kinda got someone pregnant…"
"What?! Who?! Why?!"
"No one you know… and don't worry… She got an abortion without asking."
"Oh… Shit… How are you with that?"
"Mixed."
"Yeah?"
"Yeah… I kinda accepted it after the initial news, even got excited for a certain life in the near future. Then she dropped the second news about the abortion." smiling like I do when things bother me, but I don't want to share.
"Oh my God are you ok?"
"I mean, no, but what the hell am I going to do?" ordering more shots,
"Not the end of the world… for me. Yeah I'm miserable." Laughing.

She always use to comment when I would laugh about serious things. *'It's your defensive mechanism'* she would always say. *'Duh'* I would always reply, laughing some more while looking around her head. The thing about my laughter thing is that it's not a fake laugh. I've always found the funny in shitty situations. Not to say I've never freaked out or worried about stuff. Laughing works, but it is sprinkled with middle-of-the-night panic attacks about things ahead. Those are usually funny after they pass though. It's impossible to void all worry, even though worrying is a useless trait. I've tried to abolish it, mostly by avoiding most causes - women, career, babies (until lately), etc. Laughter is my way. I've been giggling like a little girl this whole trip. She would say she could never understand how I could do it. I could never understand how I couldn't.

Hmph…

With some sort of smile we cheers.

"To no babies" mumbling *'anymore'* under my breath.

Flirtatiously appalled she hits me, smiling a little too much to herself.

I ask how things are with the boyfriend, uninterested already assuming the story. Things are *good* with drawn out emphasis on the good. That's my *'could be better could be worse'* response in girl talk - less than ideal but not horrible to the point where she's going to do something about it. It's been over a half-decade they've been together. Takes some serious happenings to break that chain of unbearable, unconditional feeling of obligation toward each other. Cheating in itself wouldn't even work. She would have to find him in bed with a friend that turned out to be a tranny that ditched plans with her that night to have sex with her boyfriend. Even then the outcome may only be one less secret tranny friend. She'd be most pissed about the plans.

Done with the catch up joke we go back to the way things were - frustratingly fun. A familiar song comes on. Drunk from the drinks I grab her hand and pull her off her stool/my lap at this point.

"What are you doing?"
"Shhhutupp"

I start dancing with her, not that I can, but feelings are a magnificent trump card. Not into it at first, she laughs a little. Giving up quickly, she starts back at me. It's been a bit since I've stood this close to a girl. I get a little turned on. We head butt dance. This turns me on even more as I loudly whisper "Well hello.." She laughs and sinks her head into my shoulder. The song ends.

"Good... we should stop anyway."

I laugh some more pretending to know what she's thinking.

"I think I need another drink." she says.

I think to myself 'she doesn't' as I wave to the bartender for another round.

This should be fun.

We start to settle regarding the moving around we're doing. No more dancing, just laughing and subconscious drunk flirting. She says something, we laugh. I say something, we laugh some more. This quickly calms down with a synchronized sigh, both catching our breath staring down at the bar. I can't look right or left for too long or else my shitty neck starts hurting.

"Wanna skip out of here?" sensing it's time to go.
"Yep" no hesitation.

I settle up. She bitches about wanting to pay for it and I just ask 'for what?'

"You're an asshole" I get in return.

First thing that jumped in my head as well. Incapable of math, I tip what I think is well over 20%. It's not surprisingly outrageously expensive. She slurs out 'well thanks' taking my arm.

"Well hello."

We stumble down blocks like a messed up homeless couple about to have sex in front of some children, both temporarily half deaf yelling point blank directly into each other's ear. She mentions something about how she could use a cigarette. It dawns on me that I haven't had one this whole time - too distracted with her to care. Now reminded, I pick up the pace to find the nearest 13 dollar pack of shitty cigarettes. I trip over myself trying to duck into a place that looks typical for cig selling. I don't want to know how much my brand is. I order a 'pack of your cheapest cigarettes'. There's a couple at the same price. I let her pick.

11.50

Could be worse.

Also could be better.

I steal a lighter and save three bucks.

We sit on the step to her building because like any normal person she doesn't like cigarette smoke in her place. I have to agree. Our arms are linked at the elbow as we smoke our bogues.

"Wanna run away with me?" exhaling a big puff of smoke.

She laughs like I'm half joking, knowing I'm half serious and then sighs...

"Oh..."

I flick my butt far into the street, put my hand to her chin and gently pull her to mine. I can feel her submission until the last moment when she pulls away.

"I can't" almost disappointed (in my mind completely).

Understandable though. She's been in her relationship longer than I want to remember. She can't just chuck that all away on a brief feeling for her stupid, quarter-life crisis ridden schmuck of a friend from college that never got the hint that nothing would ever come of them, even if there were feelings on both sides. I'm not sure what I was expecting. Must've figured it was worth a try. Either way - try and fail or no attempt at all - I'm on the road wishing she were with me. At least I know what's up now though, confirming what I refused to believe in college.

It's been a few moments since the attempt and I've gone speechless.

"...You know I just can't..." apologetic.
"Yeah I knowwww."
"I did like how you pulled me over."
"yep... not enough though."

It's good to know she is into it, but held back by stuff that's well within her control.

"You shouldn't be into that if you're happy with him."
"We have good and bad times like everyone else."
"Seems it's often bad with how much you call me drunk and upset at night."
"I know. I know. That's not right of me... I just know you're there for me.... Haven't done it in a while though."
"When I don't enjoy things I don't do them"
"Yeah..."
"Just split with me out to California"
"I can't do that."
"You can."

Things are cut and dry for me when I get all boozed up and I want something. This goes on for a while. I ask 'why?' a lot and make a bunch of what I think are good points (i.e. 'why not?!'). It's frustrating knowing that I can usually convince girls to do anything. At the same time, I never like the ones that listen. The one thing that she can't get over is the time they've been together.

"But we've been together forever..."

I remind her she's been miserable for a lot of the time. I understand the concept. I really do. Ending it would be like throwing the last 5 years of her life down the shitter. Then comes the regret of everything she missed, everything she sacrificed to make it work. She can't get those years back. If she holds on, they will mean something forever, or until it inevitably ends. I could never justify saving the last couple years at the expense of the rest of my life. Then again, things are really cut and dry for me right now.

I wish this would be a freeing chat. The kind that makes me go *Oh... Ok... Yeah... now I know... Now I'm good. I'm glad this happened.* Nope. Rather *Oh... Ok... She's still deceiving herself... She wants* me... It's just not the time... I'm the man... Time to have sex with her best friend.

That used to happen sporadically through college. I would often wake up 10 feet from her in the mornings in her roommate's bed. It was all the emotional/psychological connection I wanted with her accompanied with the physical fest I had with her roommate. It was almost exactly what I wanted. I took what was given to me. I didn't plan it that way consciously, maybe, actually subconsciously. Whatever. It was forever ago. The dark funny about it is that that wasn't the first time that sort of thing happened.

I was stuck on another girl from high school for a good length of time. It was another one of those bad timing things. She lived far away while I couldn't drive, then she transferred when I could to a boarding school even farther away. Usually it would be *out of sight out of mind* but unfortunately for me this was one time I acted a little older. We kept in touch via this and that, eluding to both of us being together eventually. I went to college, tried to keep the flow going, but who wants long distance friends freshman year of college? I forget if I was trying to get in contact with her and couldn't, or if I was pouting about her not doing that for me. Not sure what makes me angrier - her not caring to get in touch with me, or me doing the same for her. Either way her best friend came to visit with one of mine. Bla Bla Bla Smash Smashy. The next weekend my boarding school soul mate calls out of nowhere and wants to visit. She comes up with the same friend of mine. Bla Bla Bla we are lying in bed and she tells me she loves me and always has, but she knows what happened the past weekend.

Nothing happened between us physically.

That's not what bothers me.

There's nothing I can ever say to change things.

Don't have sex with the girl you love's best friend... no matter how intelligent the spite you're feeling seems.

Side note aside, I'm still on the stoop outside. Not sure how long I've been daydreaming right next to her. Her head is resting on my shoulder and her arm under mine. It'd be nice if she would tell me she hates me and go upstairs without me. Anything short of this is an invite to pursue. The nice part about this is that it's an open invitation for an undisclosed moment, the only scheduling being done when we are already there.

I was never one for party planning except inviting as many people and buying as much booze as possible.

I untangle my arm from hers and throw it around her shoulders. Tractors slip into my mind for some reason. Pulling her close I kiss her on her forehead - a neutral spot for most. It would be nice, being with her, but after something like she's been in for so long, it takes a bit to move on. I've got time yet - turn of the century invite, the Y2kiss my ass of a tease I put on myself. My luck the world would explode when it happens. Nothing like a pessimistic attitude about a fictitious situation that will never happen to put you in a good mood. I think it's time to go.

"Let's go up" she says, parting from me toward the door.
"Think I'm going to head out actually." after pausing, contemplating sex.
"What? Why? Don't be mad."
"I'm not, not at all. These cigs aren't going to smoke themselves."
"You're bitter."
"Probably. It's time to go though."

I stand up and walk backwards through my last sentence, avoiding physical contact. She likes this too much for me to stay. She doesn't get her keys out - just looks at me as I wave and turn to go. I have no direction but it's not the time to be funny and stumble back the other way, passing her with a stupid grin and a funny second hug (which would be the first in this case). Does she want me or is she smashed. She is smashed, probably not the other. Indifferent most likely.

I tell myself she is sobbing

I light a cigarette as my mind returns to my body. My heart is going fast and I'm walking the wrong way. I will get a sense of direction next millennium. Where is a cab?

"CABB!!"

The next morning is unlike the others. I feel better, well rested. It would be nice if it were due to my recent closure, but seeing that I got none, it can't be. Last night I passed out as soon as I got in the room around seven. It is 11:30. I slept for 16 and a half hours on a bed made for sleeping. I remember my dreams being really pleasant, but not them themselves. That's good. Remembering pleasant dreams makes the day the much worse.

I had a nice time yesterday. Not sure what I was expecting.

I will treat it like the rest of my time with her, a prolonged chain of happenings that if put closer together, would lead through a normal chronology of events for two people getting together.

This is the shitty part. Leaving with no one chasing after me. Driving out of this diarrhea mess of traffic, I keep looking in my mirrors hoping to see her at one angle or another, but only the homeless and other common big city staples are about. I light a cigarette. Nothing helps like slowly killing yourself - breathing out the bad and taking in the good. I can feel the smoke murdering my lungs. Breathing out is relieving. I go back for some more as I continue in the standstill of this constipated log jam of cars.

Why can't she just come with me? This is lame and unfair. The one time I want someone they do not want me. It's because of my rules. I disobeyed. I need to stop talking to myself. It makes things worse. She does not want me. Who cares? I have been through worse. Get over yourself.

The rest of the trip is forgettable. All the towns are the same and I did not feel like figuring out how to make it to the good cities - mostly because there were no lost love interests along the way. If the one from high school was anywhere out here I would have sought her out, but she is back east in DC now I believe. Should have planned this trip out a little better - mapped out all major love infatuations to zig-zag through America. I was too out of my head at the time to do so. That would have been work. I hate work. Life is work.

I want to smoke meth.

Still no stamp on my penguin card.

Only one shot. Has to be worth a year.

Wonder if there is anyone worth a year.

X

Tired of driving. Time to make the last push for the western pond. Smash through it. Ten, 20 hours, has to be done now before everything goes south. Anyway, I am close. Can smell it, I think. Might have been me rolling down the windows a little more to let in something else besides the smell of smoke and ass. It might be premature. When my family would go down to the Outer Banks I could smell the ocean a little after Maryland, not half way down. There would still be five hours left and I am there telling myself it is almost over. The thought of how much driving I have done over the last weeks scares me. Too much me time.

Seven hours, four packs of cigarettes and a quick stop on the side of the road for a self-handy and I see water. I promise myself when I get to the edge that I will just drive straight through.

I roll into a town. It is like the others except I assume people are willing to pay thousands for a closet. Tired, defeated, little bit curious and horny. For how beautiful California is supposed to be, this place has a few things in common with my ass. Stick a scenic beach cliff next to the shitty part of back home and the landlords would be twice the richer. But beaches are here and instilled from childhood is a love of the beach. Not the boardwalk ones though.

This trip has been filled with some sort of anticipation. Maybe more like uncertainty. A type of anxiety regarding getting here or away from where I was. I am not sure what the hell I have been feeling, but I have been anything but relaxed. Very similar to my childhood anticipation for the beach. In the car I could not wait to get there. Pulling up to the house I would almost shit myself for all reasons possible. I would get out and unpack by throwing my bag on some bed in the mansion. Then I would run down to the beach to find a feeling of 'ok... now what?' So much anticipation for something fabulous. There is nothing fabulous. It is the mood that is fabulous

You go to the beach to do nothing and not feel bad about it. You can do it anywhere. It works though. All the hustle and bustle for so long and there you sit with your ass in an uncomfortable chair staring at a nice replacement for your back yard.

I figure the best way to the ocean is to drive toward it. I do that. There is a lot of similarities I see from the other place but I am at the beach, the west coast, California. Nothing can touch me except my colon.

There is something like a drop off ahead. I park, falling short of my promise. I am dying and almost fall out of the car. Walking towards where I am going I look up a bunch like I am being filmed and this is the turning point, a climax.

There is a smashed bottle on the side walk. The people do not seem to care about the water. No girls have taken off their clothes yet. I might be in the wrong place. I might have circled around to Jersey. There is a sharp stabbing pain in my foot. I assume it is glass and rub it on my other leg's shin. It kind of goes away and I go on.

At the edge there is some neglected stairs going down to the beach. It would be funny if they collapsed and killed me after driving all the way out here so I skip down them with a heavy emphasis on landing with all my weight in the middle of each step. At the bottom I run to the water's surf and dig my feet into the wet sand, already have taken my shoes off sometime along the way. I reach down and touch the ground like a cross country shuttle run, but I am not heading back soon. Might be disqualified. I used to win the shuttle run in fourth grade. It got me all the ladies. I do not know what the ladies like anymore.

Not liking getting wet I trudge back up to dry sand and sit down staring at the ocean. I forget which one it is. I don't think I ever knew. Don't think I ever cared. There is really only one ocean anyway. This is nice.

I go blank for a bit. The wave sounds are the only thing running through my head. The endless ocean is endless - deep. I laugh at that. Waves come relentlessly. 'One more and I will leave' I keep telling myself. I lie to myself a couple hundred times. It works the same for bars and other times.

Now what. Never thought through what I do once I get here.

It is getting dark now. I did not think the sun set on California. Wrong once again. Oh yeah that is Alaska. I am not driving there. Heard it is nice though. There is some cigarettes in my pocket with one match. I am terrible with matches. I should bury it in the sand. It would be the same. I light it and get half the tip of my cigarette lit before it goes out.

It is full blown dark now.

I sleep on the beach.

It is nice.

I am at the beach.

There is sand in my everything and I am confused. Favorite morning so far. Thinking back to last night and my sentimentality I laugh. The stairs are longer up than down. At the top I ask the first person that does not seem to be on the harder drugs where we are. She is a lady, ugly as shit. She says it is illegal to sleep on the beach. Fighting the urge to tell her what else is illegal I ask,

"Which beach?"

She gurgles something before walking on by me.

"Thanks."

If I am where I think she said I am, then I'm not too far from my buddy from college. A couple stops down the coast. Could be a long drive. I have no idea. It could be a five hour drive and I would not notice. The last couple weeks have made driving any distance seem like a hop. I would still prefer an even shorter trip though. Traveling is not my favorite at the moment. A shower is at the top of my revised list.

I am going to set my car on fire when I get to his house.

I pull onto his street in San Diego. This is much better than where I collapsed last night. It fits the California image I had in the back of my head on the way here. Thank Christ too because I would have had to leave, probably for Alaska. Assuming parking is awful I park in the first spot I see. On my walk I count the empty spots I could have held out for. I do not care. It is nice to be on foot. Would not have minded walking from last night's beach if I knew exactly how long it would have been. It is good to walk. It still sucks though.

The blocks are a mile each. After some time I see a monstrous figure sitting on a porch smoking some sort of something. Hopefully it is a cigarette. This walking is tiring. Getting closer I see it is my friend and his 6'10 frame. One of the happiest guys I know. He knows what is important, or what is not. We are alike. There may not be that much in the world that is worth a while, but when you realize you do not have to worry about all the other stuff you start enjoying life a little better. We have never talked like this, but we are alike.

Another good friend from college who gave everyone nicknames that ended up sticking. His was 'too tall'. So I yell that over and over.

His head perks up. My shrill screams are audibly difficult. He probably thinks someone is slaughtering a cow next door. Happy cows. I yell again. This time he gets up and looks down the street. He sees me and keeps looking. I yell one last time and he finally recognizes me.

"Holy shit!"
"Yeah boyeeee."

He jumps off the porch and sprints towards me. I notice he does not have any pants on, only boxers. He catches me before I have a chance to do something. We man hug, suitable for the situation if not for his dangling 6'10 balls on my chest.

This is nice. Not the balls, but the familiar male camaraderie. No underlying motives or the awkward stages of a new friendship. It is just *'good to see you'* and right back to college. The *'what now'* feeling fades for now and I am relieved - no stomach cramps or invisible weight on my shoulders. No general consensus of *'well this isn't going to end well'* - not saying it will, but not worried for now. He brings me to the porch and throws me a beer from the cooler that is accompanying him. Natty light. Right back at school.

"No work today?"
"Dude... it's Saturday."
"Oh."

We blab back and forth about how we are doing and what we have been up to.

"I could complain."

Always gets a laugh out of people. The respectable ones respond something like 'but who would listen, right?' Always get rise out of that. He says good and explains his job with no emphasis. I explain my trip out here and how fun it is to drive so long by myself. For my job I say "living" and laugh at the stupidity. He laughs at me laughing and we both continue like assholes.

"Alright... so you just picked up and left?"
"Yep." eyes going down with a smile of *'you're going to get a kick out of this'*.
"Why? How?" expectedly asking
"Well I had, and still have, although slightly less, a ton of cash. Bar work is found anywhere. Needed a change of scenery."
"That's sweet dude."
"And I got someone bitch pregnant." I say as if talking about sports.

It does not set in on him for a brief second. That time ends with a laugh. He thinks I am joking but then sees I am not laughing.

"Wait... Seriously?!"
"Yeah but it's fine. She got an abortion after I jumped on board." smiling again.
"Holy shit dude... I'm sorry?"

"Meh... It's ok. Think I might be over it. Doesn't really matter though. Just drove across country. Let's party."
"Ok. Let me call some people."
"Yes. Some less forced companionship."

He hops on the horn. I go for another beer. Wonder if there is any booze. I am looking to make an impression on this town immediately. It is time to find my queen penguin. Preferably a blond penguin with a nice butt. Oh nice. A plastic gallon of vodka, price labeled with a sale sticker. Must be hitting the expiration date. Did not know bleach went bad. Most of the cupboards are bare, both of food and glasses. You can tell he got a real job right out of school. There are some glasses stained with hard water. I know clean when I see it and there is nothing wrong with this. The bleach vodka will get those stains right out anyway. Two and a half shots worth should be about right. I fill each up a thumbs worth, then a little more for me, then a little more for too tall. Smelling them makes me cringe, a mistake worth a laugh. He is yelling on the phone outside so I take my fresh drinks out to him.

"...so yeah you should come over he's great..."

He is talking to a girl. You don't say that to guy friends. Invites for guys is a text of *'beers now come'*. Then you forget immediately that you ever spoke to them. Girls always have the questions:

What time?
Who's coming?
Where are we going then?
Are we going out then?
Who's coming again?
Do I know them?
I'm cold!
Can I come after ____ (anything from a time to an activity that is urgent)
Can my friend (always a friend of yours) come?
Your house?
Wait... Today?
Why don't you just come here?
I'll let you know.

I shove the almost half-filled glass in his face.

"My buddy from school..." with a quizzical look on his face like he had no clue he had any liquor.

We both slug it back, immediately coughing but holding it in regardless. He continues choking as I hear the girl ask if he's alright. I am already a bit drunk so I continue laughing, eventually just laughing at me laughing.

"Well it's warmer over here… " holding back laughter with a smile.

"Alright just hit me up then." hanging up.
"Not coming."
"Fuck her... What was that shit."
"Bleach... it was on sale."
"Oh shit. I forgot I had that."
"Nice. Another?"

He goes in and brings the bottle out with him. I agree. Moving sucks. We pour another, not so deep, but deep enough, setting it in a cooler of ice. If we have to drink bleach then let it be chilled.

For the next bit or so we sit and bullshit about the stuff you think we would. He tells me about the life out here - the girls, beaches and general mindset, focusing on the legalization of pot. Everything is better out here. It is all laid back and easy. A place where I should have been my whole time. It is 75 and sunny, every day, all day, all year, all life. I like my rain but this weather is hard to argue. With every description he laughs like *yeah... unbelievable right?* I have been here for a day, already I cannot imagine being anywhere else.

My turn comes. "Well... besides the unexpected pregnancy of?" laughing obnoxiously I go on to tell about my trip. He knew the girl I stopped to see. Also knew I had a thing for her. I give my slurred speech about how *I know* she wants to be with me but cannot because of the circumstances. A tune he has heard before but not for a while. Funny that I never realize that is how it always is. Maybe it has never been the way I have thought it was. He nods politely like I am an idiot. I am. I don't notice and keep yelling. I scream about the shitty towns I have been to and how that one night that one girl came back with me.

Then I remember the Penguin Club gang.

"Oh yeah! And the Penguin Club!"
"Penguin Club?"

I explain it like it is the greatest thing ever. He looks at me like a eunuch. Going on and on about it I get a little weird. I explain how it is going to help me in regards to women. I am not going to jump into anything, especially since now I only get one shot a year.

"I had that time in my life and look where it got me... Pregnant, then not pregnant. 3000 miles later I'm here. Need to get things at least a little straight. Hell, I don't know... I'll probably smash more now..."
"Hmm." laughing "I'll start a rabbit club."
"Yeah that's what everyone says... Shot thirty?"

The sun is starting to go down. I didn't think the sun set on California. Oh wait, that's Alaska. Heard it is nice there. His friends start showing up. The girls are blond knock outs. The guys are dudes.

They all yell his name as they stroll in. Everyone always loved the 6'10 bastard.

This is nice.

He introduces me like some ruined woman searching for one last fling. I'm not ruined, only soiled. Introductions all around. I make it clear I will remember no one's name. I'm also up front about my intentions.

"I'm looking for my penguin."

He laughs and everyone else is confused. He tells them they wouldn't understand. I look at one of the blonds and respectfully disagree. The poor girl is even more confused and now a little creeped out. I laugh obnoxiously and throw everyone drinks.

Look at me... Life of the party.

It is getting chilly now - low 70's. I laugh obnoxiously some more and quack for the sound of a penguin. I believe it's a breed of duck.

The night continues enjoyably. We play college games and get over my first impression nicely. The girls are looking nice so I try my best not to hit on any of them - more successful out of the game than in. It's almost as hard as hitting on them. The drunker I get the cleverer I feel and the more I see that they want me. I sit next to a 6'10 wall to shelter me from the girls' beckoning calls.

I try to say something short after, forgetting why I switched seats in the first place. A mumbled and gargled gibberish vomits out of my mouth. Luckily for me mostly everyone is already yelling for some reason. One of the girls, cute, caught it and giggled.

Quack Quack.

"Shhhh... don't tell anyone."
"That was quite the sound attempt."
"Yeah, well, the sound was funnier than what I was saying."
"It's good I didn't make it out then."

It is time to relocate but my early strategic position is getting in the way. It is impeding me from having sex with my penguin. Probably more helping actually. I rethink and remember that whatever I think would be a good idea right now, isn't. Moving right now is too needy and pathetic - both great descriptions of myself but not what I need on my first social night. Stay calm and I will rise from adversity. That sounds wrong.

Ooops... Gotta shit... perfect...

I'm so smart.

Excusing myself I get up and leave the children circle we have formed around the coffee table, hip checking mine in the shoulder with my butt - have to throw the first punch. The rules of flirting from 4th grade shine true more than ever now - hitting, throwing things, making random sounds at them.

She smiles.

And the hustle walk back - both good and bad, the bathroom is in the back of the apartment. It is nice - boyish but clean. Sitting down I feel like I could be dividing Canada and the US - daredevils tight roping and tossing themselves over in barrels. A legit tourist attraction where visitors say 'Oh my! That's neat!'

Out of toilet paper. Not good.

Oh nice. Tissues. Even better.

Brief and uneventful. Still longer than a piss though. Cover up time. The kitchen is useful and full of shit to bring out. Hoping someone brought in the beers and booze I open the fridge. Sweet, my hopes and dreams come true - beers and booze. Not the beers from the cooler, not that it matters. I grab a few along with the plastic bottle and some plastic cups - easier than shot glasses.

I walk back into the living room, arms full of goodies more manageable than it appears. I plop down at the edge of the coffee table, conveniently next miss penguin.

"Man, you can't find anything in there.... is it shot o' clock?"

Half say no so I fill a cup for everyone. I laugh obnoxiously and stand up to give my toast, forcing everyone to join. They all groan. A few hours to wear out my welcome is pretty respectable. A moment of silence comes with me smiling as if I just pulled a joke on them. After a deep breath I continue:

>I would like to thank all of you for tolerating me, especially you my tall friend. You are the tallest

gentleman I know, not to mention one of my good friends. As for the ladies, who shall remain nameless, you are all beautiful. Gentlemen, also remaining nameless, you are all probably good looking as well... I'm not one to judge. Quack Quack

Kicks are had from my indignant behavior. Maybe they aren't used to it, or maybe they are since they laughed. Either way, they are laughing. Things are going well, especially with the one to my right, the girl that thinks it is funny when I fart noises out of my mouth. Our legs are touching and she doesn't seem to mind. In cramped spaces like this body contact is not a mystery, but you can avoid it if needed. She likes it, or she sees my other leg starting fires with the guy next to me and deems me unthreatening. Not important now. What is important is that she is feeling something. However it may just be the booze - those shots were a three finger pour.

We are getting louder and move on to a new game, the bowl game. The rules are not important. What is important is at the end of each round the loser has the choice of either drinking a mixture of everyone's drink or taking off some clothes. I prefer both.

A couple rounds roll by and half are naked. The one next to me is shirtless with a bra. I haven't lost yet but my pants are off anyway - trying to make her feel better about herself. Me being pant-less usually has that effect.

"Oh shit I'm going to be completely naked!" another girl screams after losing again.
"I wouldn't worry about it." I say.
"That's because you get to see my tits!"
"That's exactly why I wouldn't worry about it."

I don't worry about it

Everyone laughs and agrees, regardless of my reasoning. I offer to match and take off my shirt before she says anything. It comes back to me how fat I have gotten over the last couple weeks.

"Well hello there..." my girl says staring straight at my unfortunate body.

"Hey!" buying time "I like food! Take off your bra!"
"Yeah!" a guy screams on the other side of the table, me just noticing he's completely naked standing on the arm of the couch holding his junk with a bright pink hat.

That snuck up on me. I laugh obnoxiously, glad she stopped focusing on my gut. You can't put your clothes back on mid-game. It's a rule.

She hits me and pokes my fat belly. I yell obnoxiously loud with a rasp. It startles everyone. I don't feel embarrassed but my body turns bright red anyway - thought I kicked this in high school. Guess not.

"Holy shit you're bright red" she quacks
"Yeah, I have mood skin."
"Oh really?! What's red?!"
"Horny."

Everyone laughs. I laugh at them laughing at me so often. It's nice being in a new group of people - reminds me I'm not dull as shit. I do feel silly. It's like telling dick and fart jokes to 4th graders. I should rattle off a list of female reproductive organs. That would slay them. I like being funny, but not the funny guy. Too much.

"Horny huh?" from a girl I can't remember being there before "What other colors do you show?"
"Um... white, purple, grayish, translucent... tope... green sometimes too."
"And what do those colors mean?" my penguin asks.
"Oh... They all mean horny."

Laughs. I think this is funny too so there is a dumb smile on my face. I start laughing. My girl leans in and whispers 'That's good to know.' She is really close and she breathes in my ear. I get terrible chills and shake violently.

Being extra large with extra large attributes, my large friend hears this and elbows me harder than he probably realizes. It is a little blatant because whats-her-face has a stupid I-can't-believe-he-heard-that look on her face. We are both naked so the feelings pass quickly. He is mostly naked as well but I could not give less of a shit about him and his three legs at this point.

The time is passing like we are all drunk or something or some shit. If anyone had any intention to go out they have forgot about it or don't care to anymore. I never really cared what we were going to do, especially now because I think I know what I'm going to do.

The bowl game is getting old so truth or dare is suggested. We had things right in 4th grade. Life is cancer - it gets less enjoyable as you go and in most cases you're just waiting around to die. I want to play truth or dare as much as possible, get naked as much as possible and a bunch of other things.

"I dare you to make out with him."
"I dare you to make out with her."
"I dare you to give him a lap dance."

This goes on for a bit until everyone has each other's mouth diseases.

It is my turn.

"I dare you" squeezing homegirl's thigh "to race me over there..." pointing away from where we are sitting.

Her head dips down in what I think is disappointment and probably embarrassment because I just forced her to reject me in front of everyone. That's ok. I can wait until everyone passes out so I can masturbate on the couch. Then out of somewhere she jolts up and sprints over there. Drunk and not ready I get up and start to chase after her at the same time, tripping over a chair and falling flat on my stupid drunk horny face. It's alright though - fat guts have impact absorbing qualities. My body turns a horny red still in only my boxers. I stumble up and after her, waving bye to the rest.

I have lost her.

"Hellooo!? I didn't dare you to play hide and seek!"

The place isn't too too big. My tall friend has to duck through some doorways. It is also very linear so I can effectively look while walking to the back. I grab a shot and a beer through the kitchen. This is my one shot for the year. Better make it last.

"Where the fuck are you?"
"I'm in here you drunk asshole."

Ahh. A familiar mating call.

She is in the office. Neat. The lights are off and I can only see the faint outline of a futon and a blanket smudge. Must be her. I go to rip my pants off but they are already gone, left with the mutually forgotten others in the living room.

"Well hello my penguin queen."
"What?!"
"Nevermind."

Quack Quack

I dream of love interests from lost opportunities.

I come to, slowly forgetting what I was just dreaming about. It feels like I'm still with someone. Half asleep and half drunk I hope it's a woman. A stream of light is coming through the blinds. I sneak a peek at her. I have dried glue in my eyes. I like picking it out. This girl kinda wakes up from me rustling around. She rolls over to face me. I would say she looks miserable but that might be a reflection. I have no recollection of her personally. I remember people coming over but no faces, only bodies, the shitty parts like shoulders and guy ass.

"Well hey."
"..." laughing after her silence.
"What? Poor performance?"
"Huh... no..."
"Yes!"
"Don't get excited... There was no performance."
"Even better! No babies!"
"What did happen? Did I fall asleep with my head between your legs?"
"Not quite. You apparently in love with a girl from college."
"Oh... That's nice I got into that."
"And how you bang the best friends of all the girls you fall in love with."
"Yeah that happened a few times... Bet that was entertaining."
"Not really."
"Oh don't be annoyed... Maybe I'm trying to break the chain."

She fake laughs at that.

"So no baby mama sudden abo-bo"
"Huh?"
"Good. Never mind. Have any hot friends?"

She doesn't want to laugh at this but she does anyway. I think she thinks I'm an asshole. Doesn't seem to be faulting me for it though. I take the cheap laugh

"Bye." heading for the door.
"Byyyeeee." rolling over and closing my eyes.

The room is completely filled with sun. It is truly awful. Forcing myself to get up, I get up. Out in the kitchen there's a pot of coffee brewing. Grabbing the biggest liquid holder I gesture towards my new roommate for some. He laughs when he looks at me. I don't have to imagine how terrible I look. Pouring me some coffee he says "Heard you had a good night..."

"Fact! I did not tell her about the abortion. I'm making progress."

We laugh and head to the porch. I ask him how his night translated. He says he smashed one of the girls but it is a regular thing so it's no big deal.

"Oh yeah." I say
"Yeah?"
"Can I crash here for a bit? I don't want to go home."
"That's cool man. I think you marked your spot anyway."
"Just with tears."

I don't think this over much. I must have known in the back of my head that that was the only real option, or the only one I would accept. There's nothing back east for me - no job, no girl. My family is all there but come on, need to get out sometime. If no one ever left their family we would all still be in Africa. My dad has told me on many occasions to 'get the fuck out.' At least for a while. My mom cries when I go on vacation without her but understands leaving is a good idea.

"Gunna get a job?"
"Probably should. I'll get some bar job."
"That'll work... I know some people at some bars."
"Neat... Yeah... That should work."
"I'll check work too. See if there's any openings"
"Oh yeah... we did major in the same thing."
"Yeah..."
"Real job. That'd be weird. Tell them I have plenty of bar experience."
"Haha... ok."
"Well this deserves a celebration! Drinks!"
"It *is* almost noon."

We go for lunch at one of the bars he was talking about, O'something-or-others. I won't remember it, even if I do get a job here. It's not too far, couple blocks from his house, a nice walk on a nice day, so a nice walk indefinitely. The place is big but sectioned off like a good bar should. The employees are hot, especially the girls - all about the age I still think I am. The hostess seems miserable. I hold my tongue. We sit at the bar. It is busy for some reason. I remember people out here are more pro-actively inactive, going other places besides their living rooms to do nothing. My kind of people. I am introduced to the bartender and a footnote version of my story is told. The bartender, who's name I'll have to get again later, says they are hiring I say 'sweet' and order shots for anyone who cares.

We eat, drink and have some fun. It's barely past noon so I try not to make a scene at my new potential place of work. For the better part of the duration my efforts pay off. Eventually I ask the bartender what the deal is with the hostess. She has brown hair, weird. He says she has a boyfriend of forever and it is long distance. I smile, laugh obnoxiously and turn around to check her out. She catches me, I yell 'oh shit!' and turn back around.

That went well.

I say aloud 'it's time to go before I shoot my shot before I even start here.' He understands, I think, and agrees. He says there are a couple bars on the way back we can stop. I have no reason to doubt him so I'm thinking 'perfect'.

A couple people from last night meet up with us for a few brews. Little Sunday Funday. The duck doesn't come out, whats-her-face that intimately witnessed my blackout emotional love break down. Must have work early or something. Will probably have work early every time I'm around now. I can't remember exactly what she looks like. I'm told she is attractive. Meh. I will put her in the cankles territory so I don't think about her.

The topic of conversation is last night, especially my now publicly known pseudo take down - great plan, executed poorly down the stretch. Love stories of other women don't suffice for aphrodisiacs out here. So much to learn.

We drink for the rest of the day. Most retire early because they have jobs. Too tall stays up with me for a bit until he finally needs some rest. I stay up for a bit more until I blackout and stumble into the house.

My days here have been coming in nicer and nicer. I still have a pit in my stomach. That should leave with time. Change is unsettling, especially when it is just sideways to better scenery. Life is better though. Sometimes I forget ever starting back east.

Work is nice. The restaurant industry doesn't vary much from gig to gig - subtle differences but other than that they are all identical. Some places you can drink while working, some like when you show up on time, some have hotter employees than others. I'm at O'something-or-others from that one Sunday outing. He checked at his work with no success - not too excited to hire a three-year-out college grad with extended bar experience. Oh bummer. No lab work for me.

It has been about two weeks since I started. Everyone is nice and laid back. I still don't know most people's names except for the hostess. There's a few girls all named the same, all smokin' hot so they are easy to remember. My job is mindless. I clock in as a server's assistant because servers need a lot of assistance. My street title is food runner. My trainer was the old food runner that happened upon a job through a string of lucky contacts. He explained the job quite nicely:

You give people their food.
No chat
No side work
No bullshit
Nobody realizes that you make the most out of anyone so keep your stupid mouth shut.

No complaints by me, but naturally I don't believe him - I have been alive long enough to know better. It doesn't really matter. I'm assuming I'll at least get some sort of income and my rent has been generously placed at a couple hundred a month. If dude man turns out true good for me.

It turns out that it is a pretty great set up. I work less than 30 hours a week and the money is what my predecessor said. The only negative is no weekends for me, but that is assumed going into it. The staff rocks out almost every night and for the most part are accepting of me. The hostess I noticed on my original visit is 20 and is still in school two hours away. Also, her boyfriend sucks so that doesn't really help. I am going to ask her to hang out one of these weekends.

Trudging through the back entrance on a Sunday morning I realize that this is going to become a staple riddled with head and body aches from the night before. In spite of this, I'm always on time, always arriving at noon on the dot. People think It's because I'm a hard dedicated worker. I know it is because Sundays are one of the few days the hostess works. I walk up the back stairwell filling the air with *perfume de whiskey y cheap beero*. Three steps through the door and there is already two comments on my general appearance and one on my mixed scent of brut and booze. It doesn't bother me, just need some gum to hide my rancid sub-vomit breath. There's two POS touch screens to clock in with - one in the front and one in the back. The hostess stand is in the front.

"You look beautiful." she yells as I am halfway to the front.
"Thank. You. Bitch... Must be my beauty sleep."
"Might want to take a beauty nap this afternoon." laughing, fixing my hair and collar before I check in.

If I wasn't interested in her I would be annoyed like I am with the others, but I am so I take it as consensual flirting. I would also allow it for a nice butt. Looking like shit is a great ice breaker, like sweat pants at a bar. We jibber jabber back and forth before I walk away in the middle of one of her sentences.

"...and... ummm... thanks for LISTENING!!"
"You were boring me.." without turning around.

Another perk of my job is that I can sit on a stool and watch T.V. until there is an order up. Sundays have been dick for me so far - guess that first time here was a fluke. Either way I get my hour of Sportcenter in while waiting for customers to come join me. I hate them all before they come in. My motivation on Sundays is the hostess. Work is much more enjoyable with her walking back and forth in front of me seating guests. On the way there I smile and wink, on the way back I say stupid stuff about them to make her laugh.

The crowd starts rolling in making her almost run back and forth. She makes faces varying with the variety of people she parades around. I laugh and make comments on how the old and fat people fall behind a few car lengths struggling with her pace. Sometimes they ask questions - I have never heard so many one word answers from a girl who looks so sweet, when she is actually portraying, 'Go Fuck Yourself.'

It becomes a joke between us - how we hate everyone that steps through the doors. It is kind of a joke - we both do actually hate everyone that walks through the doors. I will take any back and forth with her at this point. At least her boyfriend is far enough away to irregularly come around. Absence makes the heart grow fonder - fonder of who you are around all the time. The key is to stay unthreatening. Most girls believe guys can genuinely want to hang out and be friends. What they don't know is that they are 100% wrong. I swear only 5% of women have seen *When Harry Met Sally*.

The rest of the day goes like I like - a little slot, letting us flirt with little interruption. We play 'Guess who the next schmuck will be' and make fun of customers before they step inside. We laugh like we are freshly in love. Coworkers ask if there is anything going on between us. I just sigh and loudly moan without eye contact, writing something on the server calendar that doesn't make any sense - mostly a lot of cross hatching. They also ask her. I imagine she responds something about her boyfriend, avoiding the actual question, but no one really notices. She does tell one of the girls that she thinks I'm cute. I can deal with that for now. There is no hurry.

The shift is coming to an end. She is finishing up some bullshit at the hostess stand. I have no bullshit, or anywhere to be so I chit-chat with her. I am not kidding anyone, I would do the chit-chat even if I had to urgently be somewhere. We laugh about how stupid someone is. I ask what she is up to now. It's so much better than coming right out and asking her to do something. Sensing where I'm heading with this...

"I have to move my grandmother out of her house the rest of the day..."

Not knowing if she's lying or not I appreciate her pre-emptive rejection.

"What are you doing?" she asks
"Not sure... Have the rest of the day off... Might start boozin"
"Huh... Goood... Get them bitties for me."

She says these type of things to me now and then. I'm never quite sure how to respond. Usually I say something about blonds and no cankles. She laughs. I hope she's hoping I'm not serious, that I may be holding out for her. That might be the situation. I'm definitely not not pursuing anyone on her account. I can't say I wouldn't be receptive though.

She likes talking with me, but still, I don't want to annoy her. I leave wishing her a *have fun* as I put on my sunglasses and back out the front doors thinking "Come with me you bitch!" She looks down and starts writing something on the podium - hopefully some crosshatching.

Back East there would be days that were gorgeous. Sunny and perfectly hot, no clouds in the sky and girls everywhere I looked. These days you would have to party outside. If you couldn't get off work, you would go in drunk. Obnoxiously loud music was a must. Everyone within a mile would have to hear. This attracted the females from all around. In college we had a front lawn on the main path students would walk. It would be an all day party starting as soon as the first one of us woke up.

The best.

Here, every day is like that. I get outside and the sun forces my eyes shut even with glasses. A deep breath brings me full circles. Things still aren't near perfect but on days like this I often forget.

Beers?

Getting back to the house, I see too tall and the rest way ahead. They are all on the porch as shirtless as each can get. Beer cans litter the steps and railings. A smile comes to my face as a beer closely follows flying in the air as I walk up to everyone.

Coming out here was a good idea.

One of the girls takes off the shorts over her bathing suit...

Really good idea.

This whole gig isn't surprising. The gang comes over often. I have actually been remembering that one girl's name. It is something regional but with a foreign nickname. She is hot and has spoke with me sober on a few occasions which helps the case. It is kind of weird. We have been hanging out in the group, but enjoying each other more than the rest. There has been nothing more than that - no awkward exchanges or inadvertent physical bumps. I do not even have her number. I may have given her mine, but I choose to think she lost it, or that it was one of the dudes. I can't remember. This weather goes straight to my liver.

I walk up the stairs to the porch, subconsciously looking for my social companion. She is not outside so I pretend to have to piss, not that anyone would care if I went and looked for her - can't be too needy. She is nowhere to be found on the way back to the bathroom - I have since realized I need to shit. I am a little disappointed. Maybe I missed her outside. Maybe I will call her. Maybe I will get her number next time.

My bowel movement is brave and loyal.

I head back out, done with my beer and needing something a bit stronger. I stop in the fridge on the way. Some slimy vodka, OJ and sprite will do for now. Stirring my concoction I walk back out to paradise.

Right out the door someone smacks me right in the head. Still slightly pissed about not finding her, I turn with some rage with a mean look. My death face melts into a smile.

"You think you are funny don't ya?!"
"Yep." she replies.

Her smile gives away that I would let her do anything and get away with it.

Looking her up and down I would like her to sit on my face. I smile thinking of what I am about to do.

"What?!" in retreat.

I check to my right to see if it's clear. Seeing so, I smack her drink out of her hand as hard as I can. Everyone turns to us not knowing what's going on as we both break into laughter. Everything is fine in the eyes of everyone so no one cares and loses interest.

"You're dry. Can I get you a drink?" I ask.
"You're an ass... Yes."

We walk together inside and bullshit about what she wants. I pour a ridiculous one and hand it to her. She laughs, pours half of it in my cup and smacks me playfully across the face.

"Thanks... Mine was weak anyway."

She turns away. I can tell she is smiling by the raise in the back of her hairline. She mixes something at the counter. I come up from behind her and wrap my arms around to mess up whatever the hell she is doing. She elbows me in the stomach - half playing but mostly really pissed. Good to know she can take care of herself. At the very least elbow perverts in the stomach very well.

We laugh and face each other for no reason. Her hands are joined around her cup in front of her breasts, no way for my chest to make contact. Total bullshit. My hands are on the counter, trapping her in a box of counter, arms and my atrophied chest (no one works out here and is naturally gorgeous... I can't keep up so I don't try).

She is staring downwards, I'm not sure at what. My eyes are on her cleavage - popping out all over the place from her arms and my bird chest. I lightly head butt her on the top of her head. My hands come off the table half way, now half on her lower back - I am terrified of rejection so I have to hedge my passes and see what she does, like I don't take everything any girl does as a pass at me.

I am lost in that thinking.

Her hands slip from between us and down my sides to rest where I should be wearing a belt. She cannot find it and I can tell she is delightfully confused.

"This weather is making me fat! No need for belts!" dumbly.
"I think you look fine."
"You must be a bit blind."

She smiles a little. Not as much as I would like but I tell myself she is holding back. She redeems herself with toe-raises. I think I may be on the same level now.

"Well hellooo..." still searching for the right level.

I move my hands up her back, then down, then up. I had too much coffee at work. Her thumbs are down the sides of my belt-less waist. I am turned completely on. It has been a while and I feel like I am in fourth grade with dad's porn again. I remember girls have butts. She has a butt! A nice one too! My hands migrate down there and squeeze like there is a stress ball in both. She perks up with an 'oh!' and smiles with no teeth. I plop her on the counter and regret it since my hands are forced to let go. Her legs are around my waist and tightening. I make the manliest squeal I can and wonder why I'm not kissing her.

This is not too bad of a mix though. Girls are the yang to us guys' yin. Where guys want things fast and easy and immediate, girls want to be teased, drawn out and bored to death until they can't stand it. Girls also love assholes, where guys love girls that don't annoy them when they are doing stuff.

I am thinking about all this while perfectly placing my hands wherever they are now. She may be getting a little anxious now. Her hands are off my stationary hips and now split between my back and neck. Don't remember that happening but I don't remember most of the good things, human nature - never remember the good things. My dad was sick one day and passed out through the time he was supposed to pick me up from school. I remember that day, but not one of the other 4,000 days when he promptly picked me up on time. If I were tested on if my dad ever picked me up from school, it would make false reading because I would have to guess if he ever did or not.

And this is the type of stuff I think about when a hot chick has her legs wrapped around me.

"Oops! Oops! Sorry! Sorry! Just going to the bathroom." a passerby says while passing by.
"Pee! Out! Side!" I yell.
"I can't I'm a girl!"
"When are you she-critters going to stop using that excuse?"
"She-critters?!"
"Nevermind."

Knowing that girl will be back through we disconnect and act like people again. She hops off the counter and grabs her drink, heading back out. I think about how sweet it would be to have her back on the counter again. I reach out and catch her arm, spin her around dangerously and kiss her with some pre-teen passion - cracking our teeth together but holding out long enough so she knows I have done this before. She finally concedes and joins in. It is nice for a second or three until she stops as if we are at a concert and she just realized she is getting finger blasted in front of a thousand people. She gives me a look that I translate as *why not sooner?!* I smile without teeth and chuckle under my breath like we just had consensual sex against her better judgment.

Another day in paradise

The next morning is less than delightful. I cannot talk and I think someone shit in my eyes. I mumble some raspy profanities. No work today so I have no idea what time it is. I go out to get a glass of water and go take a piss. The everlasting cycle. My phone is on the bathroom sink because that's where it belongs. Knowing there are no messages for me, I check quickly. There is a text from an unknown number.

- Hey! Had fun last night... Sorry I had to go but work is a bitch in the morning.

That answers my next question. No pooty for me. I am glad she had fun. I don't remember much except the nice make out in the kitchen. That was nice - haven't felt an ass like that in some time. Felt good. Should I text back is the question now. I haven't really done the phone thing in a little while. Being me is tough. I wonder do I do it. Oh yeah... Just type the first thing that comes to mind.

I wonder if we messed around any more later in the evening. My pee is normal and brown so I am going with no. My penguin is still roaming alive and well. Hmm. I'm going to have to have perfect drunk dick for that. Nothing some Jameson and shitty beer can't handle. Let's hope it still works.

Jesus.

I need to get out of the house and go for a run or something.

I turn the TV on and start thinking about a decision that has crept up on me. Not so much a decision but an annoying fact. This girl is into me. I'm almost sure that it is not my bulbous ego either but rather a concrete progression as I have described before. Then there is the other from work who seems to be into me but has a boyfriend of forever. Of course she's the one I think about at odd times - peeing, taking out garbage, not during but after punishing myself.

I get the feeling she hates her boyfriend. That's not the problem. The problem is the forever long she has wasted with him which will feel even more lost if they break up. She will never get those years back. If it culminates into something half bearable then those shitty years will mean something. She will have something to show for it, even if it is just a kid that hates the dad a little bit more than her and a nice couch.

I need a nap.

I turn on something lame, lowering the sound so I can fall asleep. A couple minutes later for the 1000th time, I come to terms with the fact that I can't fall asleep with anything on ever and turn the TV off.

I sleep for a few hours and feel worse when I wake up. Going outside will help. I do that and grab a beer from the cooler that has been there since I got here. It is my day off and I want to drink. It may be early evening. I have no idea but I know its beer:30.

So they are both smokin' hot. The one is into me and has blonder hair - minus/plus. The hostess is flirty and a tease by default, leaving an insurmountable mountain of deeply rooted bullshit to overcome - plus. Why fall in love with a girl that will drop everything for you when you can go after a girl that most likely has no interest at all. Second guessing yourself and everything you do all the time gets fun after a little bit.

I should not listen to me this time. I have never steered me well, always ending, or endlessly lingering, with a pile of questions and alternative scenarios of better situations running through my head.

Must be drunk because I think that's witty and want to write it down.

I scan the porch as if there would be something to write with. I am disgusted that there isn't anything to write with here. Meh. I will remember it. Too good to forget. Well, maybe I should write it down just in case.

I get up to go inside, open the door and forget why I got up.

The choice is simple in two ways - who I should go for and who I will go for. I wish I had shittier parents. *'Just settle'* would be better than *'you can do anything'* right now. Or if I wasn't stubbornly competitive. Or if I wasn't exactly like every other asshole in the world that wants what he can't have.

I interrupt myself and text back.

- Well hey!... I as well had a good night too! We should probably do something sometime together or something1

Sent.

Upon review I realize I sound like a drunk ten-year-old. I'm glad that along with the lack of further reflection of who to choose, I also barred myself from editing my streaming thoughts of nonsense.

- Haha... Yeah I'd like that

Who ever said self-neglect is a bad thing - me a moment ago. I have mixed feelings about myself, along with everyone else I think.

That aside...

I got a date. Kinda. Sorta.

- how 'bout tonight?

No time like the present. Hurray for getting carried away with things.

She laughs via text again. I imagine a laugh of '*ok it's a little funny but stop typing like an idiot*' and agrees to tonight. We iron out the details throughout the day. I try to stop sounding like an idiot.

I crack open another beer realizing I've drank more than enough to carry on my drunk from last night and decide to cool it. There is nothing like showing up hammered to a date.

I am picking her up. I should clean out my car - I think it is still a colon from the trip out.

There are about a thousand bottles of water, beer and piss along with enough empty packs of cigarettes to make me second guess my habit. There is some cigarettes left in one. I light some up and smoke all of them. Part of me wants to do something artsy with all the empty packs. I get over that quickly.

I am still smoking the cigarettes when I take a break and sit on the hood. It is nice and I have a movie moment while staring at the horizon, the one that makes it California and think about women. It's pleasant. I don't want to leave. I think I fall asleep for a little but I'm not sure. It does not matter except that my door is open the whole time. I get up, close the door and head inside hoping to sober up a little more.

We go to a taco place - Taco Lou's. It is a nice place and they don't screw up the few things they make. Mexican places are good spots for dates - both have to eat with their hands and get a little slovenly. She seems like the type that would start a food fight, should work as I think. We sit in a secluded part of the restaurant, kinda romantic except for the finger foods.
She orders beef and lettuce wrapped in something and I order chicken and lettuce wrapped in something else. When it comes I just stare. It's huge, so is hers. We laugh like we are supposed to. I ask if she minds if I use a fork. "Why would I?" She replies.

The margaritas start flowing right away. My drunk comes back quickly. She sucks them down quicker than I do. She surpasses me and my drunk, she controls it well though. We laugh a lot and get louder with each bout. Dinner is finished with limited casualties on all fronts. The bar is next.

Hello bar.

We stick to the theme and stack some tequila shots between the floofy margaritas. We both are full blown hammered. I ask if she wants to get out of here, not specifying anywhere else, but she blindly agrees commenting on how it is probably time anyway - was probably time when dinner was done.

I have been taking it easy for the last half hour or so. I even got a water when she wasn't looking. I'm completely smashed. The drive isn't too too far. We should be fine.

Driving home I time the green lights so I can drift most of the way. A kid jumps out in front of me on a stupid fixed gear and scoots by. I don't see him at all but he is going fast enough so that I only I know how close he came to death. I don't react at all - good in this situation because I would have swerved and killed him.

"That would've been really bad" laughing.

I turn to her wondering why she isn't saying something only to find her asleep and drooling. I like my chicks drooling but only half asleep so they can day dream about someone more handsome while we screw around - unselfish as usual. It is basically one road to her house. She wakes up when I slow for her turn.

"Good morning."
"Oh... Sorry. Not used to staying out late during the week."
"You want me to drive around a little more so you can get your rest?"
"Shut up."

There's a bunch of silence. We both sigh from '*now what*' or to get oxygen in so neither chucks on the other. I slowly, most likely not as slow as I think, lean over to eat her face. She quickly, probably not as quick as I think, pounces on me across the center console. My hands swoop for her butt. I missed it... as in I wanted it while it was gone. Hers are squeezing my face like a fat infant. My hands slide in down the back of her jeans for some no bars contact as we are each trying to make out with the back of the other's skull. It is really great until I realize how tight her belt is. So excited for the touching, but between the carpal tunnels and the choked circulation the act is worthless short of the fact that it is happening. A few moments of these escapades transpire until both my arms start to go numb. I roll my shoulders back hoping that my arms are still attached and follow.

"Ow."
"What?" letting go of my red swollen cheeks.
"Why is your belt so tight?!" shaking my hands for feeling
"So my pants stay on!"
"Well that's stupid."
"Oh stop. I'm not that type of girl."
"Of course not." thinking '*I've never met that type in my life*'.
"Shut up!"
"What?!"

Another *'what now'* moment passes.

"I would invite you in but I have work tomorrow and I'm exhausted."
"That's fine. I wouldn't have anyway."
"Oh really?!"
"Not that type of girl."

We go back to a good bye make out repeatedly interrupted with *'ok I really need to go'*. Each face mash interval shrinks shorter and shorter. Her doors opens. We make out some more. She steps out and comes in with the back breaker. She tastes like sugar and tequila. I prefer my women reeking of whiskey but the affection feels nice regardless.

I drive home one-eying it while digging through the back seat for some cigarettes. I have no eyes on the road but I think I see something behind the passenger seat. Matches are around somewhere but thankfully I see a lighter. I would absolutely die right now if I had to light a match. I light up and take a huge breath like I just finished a marathon. My body is relaxed and my mind drifts. I think of the douche bag boyfriend and glorify myself in an imagination of me making jokes at his expense that fly way over his head. She would laugh (because we would all be together for some reason) and roll her eyes but he wouldn't notice, just me, because he's a douche.

I'm glad she has work tomorrow - no need to rush anything. It always sucks seeing someone in your group. Unless you get married, it's never the same - if it stays something at all. She is hot though. Bah! I should have chucked on myself to show her how drunk I was/am. Then she would have invited me in and we would be naked right now. Decisions - never good or bad until rectified as such. I'm horny. I don't know how anyone does this Penguin Club shit. Must be some sorts of gods or something - gods of abstinence... lasted only one generation. The power to slay but the choice to not.

Quack Quack.

This week is busy - I work four days. I drink a lot. I banter with my soon to be pseudo girlfriend but she is busy during the day while I work the hours at night. Like I said - no rush. Saturday morning rises in a thick haze of exuding Jameson sweat and some diarrhea. I have to be at work in seven minutes. I find my work clothes from the night before crumbled in a ball and put them on. I think of quitting but the hostess is scheduled today.

It feels like 5:30 and I want to die. I would say I need a real job, but then that feeling would be an everyday reality. However, I wouldn't have to move right now. But then again, I wouldn't see her. I act like

I'm going to do something about anything. I don't want a real job with responsibilities above going and retrieving. I'd rather rarely smile and have people think I'm deep when actually I'm just hungover and mildly depressed.

My shirt smells like cat piss. It is going to take a lot of lemons to cover this smell. There are sweat rings on my shirt. I will wipe them down with water when I come in the back way to work. It's sunny and awful. If the sun would rise at an appropriate time I truly believe this would be a place of paradise.

Walking into work is enjoyable. At least everyone has a hangover like me. The only difference is...

"Dude you look like shit!"

...Everyone likes pointing mine out.

"Thanks!"

I ignore most with a mild grunt or moan as I go to clock in at the front like the desperate pervert I am. She has already been there for an hour or so, not really sure and it doesn't really matter.

"Looking beautiful this morning." without looking at me
"How do you want to die?" happy because when she comments on my shittiness it is ok.
"Brutal rape homicide." no smile.
"Read my mind." also no smile
"Well that's wha...."

I leave in the middle of her sentence. She throws a piece of chalk that flies over my shoulder and lands in front of me. I step on it and keep walking. One of the other servers comments on a stupid smile that found my face.

"Think of something funny?" knowing exactly why I'm smiling.
"Yeah!" smacking the stack of bread baskets out of her hand as I keep walking.

I have a stoop at the top of the kitchen stares placed in front of one of the TVs. I sit and stare at sports for a bit. Every time she walks by I make comments and throw stuff at her. When it is slow she stops and chats with me about stupid customers and how hungover I am. She's gorgeous but I try not to stare too much. It's hard when the only thing I want to do is have her ass cheeks in my mouth. She feeds my crush consistently to my frustration. She never talks about her boyfriend - he's a douche.

The day continues like this - smiling and laughing when she's walking toward me, staring and drooling as she proceeds past me. I try to convince myself against her saying things like *'you only want her because you don't have her'*, countering with *'only one way to find out'*. It always ends with *'you're an idiot stop talking to yourself'*. She has the butt to drive a man schizophrenic. I'm fine though.

'Sure you are.'
'Yup.'
'Just Kidding I think.'

But yeah... I like working with her. It doesn't suck so bad. It sucks when the others ask if there's something going on between us and I have to yell loudly *'NO!'* I think so, but I know there's nothing going on. "Something" would only be misinterpreted flirting on my part. The shitty part for me is that she has the luxury of just saying no and it being believable. When I say no it is all dramatic and obvious that I'm in love with her. I've only really liked two girls in my life and I had sex with both of their best friends. Bordering on three I'm wondering when I will meet the best friend. Hope she's blond.

Break time is close. Saturday's are short about an hour, so not much can be done. Maybe I will ask her to get some coffee, some more because we have both slammed about 10 cups. I'm going to ask. Some answers anticipated are followed:

"Go fuck yourself."
"Our little flirty back-and-forth doesn't mean anything and I don't, nor will I ever like you as more than some comic relief at work"

Thankfully girls are never this blunt - not until you force them to be - and even then they don't mean it... at least from my experiences.

"Hey wanna grab coffee in our break."
"Uhhh... Go fuck yourself."
"Not enough time."
"Then yes."

Easy enough - in the next five minutes we are cut and off. There's a place around the corner in the sun. Good comment - everything is in the sun

I need a beer.

They don't offer beer so I get my tenth cup of coffee on the day. Someone told me once that coffee is bad for you. I hope that is not true. She gets a coffee and a cookie. I didn't think of getting a cookie. I want one now.

"I' m eating that."

"Like shit you are."
"Yes it is."
"...?"

We sit off to the side. She puts her stuff down and goes to get creamer. I take her cookie and eat the entire thing before she gets back. She doesn't notice at first but then does and threatens to kill me. I don't believe her.

We make small talk - stuff about her school and my general lack of direction and motivation. Should I ask her about her boyfriend? I think it would be normal - not like I'm asking about her last period cycle (often a topic I have to fight from bringing up).

"Any shows coming up?"
"Yeah I..."

Instead of asking questions I don't care about and not listening to the answers I should probably just ask what I about what I want to know. Chances are good that she would not mind venting about how shitty he is, or she does because it's me, or she is completely happy with him and I'm playing psycho right now. How do I bring it up without seeming like I care? Maybe if I stare into her eyes I can force her to talk about it.

"Are you alright?" she asks
"Yeah why?"
"Look's like you are going to throw up."
"Caffeine poisoning."

We talk while I continue to wonder about her boyfriend.

Finally...

"Something something something... So how's your dude friend?"
"My boyfriend?"
"Yeah that."

She sighs like I was her safe haven away from thinking of all that stuff, up until now. She starts reluctantly explaining, almost apologizing to someone about the whole thing. I'm not sure why but I may understand. It is the same shitty story. She doesn't say it's shit, but from what she says it is apparent. Things like distance and the infrequent visits, frequently ruined by arguments and resentment for the whole situation. I say things like '*yeah it's tough*' and other phrases that, with the correct emphasis, could be answers to any statement by anyone. This entire time I want to smack her in the face and say '*BE WITH ME YOU ARE BEING SO STUPID!*' I don't say this. She isn't telling me the little reasons they stay together - little moments of chivalry that normally go unnoticed in a regular relationship of two respectable people. They happen every couple weeks and come in stupid forms - *'Well he didn't throw the trash on the living room floor today'*, *'He paid his part of the mortgage from March... only three months late this time.'* These stupid things keep terrible relationships going for years past due. Instead of countless moments enjoyed with each other creating a rich and rewarding life, it's duct taped together with dog shit - *'at least we didn't fight today.'*

The break ends and we both sigh - her from relief and me from thinking *'Marry me you stupid asshole.'*

"Ready?"
"Yeah."

Dinner is busy. We don't get to flirt with each other. It's almost worse than when she is not here at all. When she's not here I can forget about her. Nights like tonight I'm forced to see her but without interaction. I don't like it but I take it. I manage to throw stuff at her and poke her when she walks by. Someone asks me "What's going on with you two?" I groan loudly and smack the bread baskets out of the girl's hand.

It's getting close to the end. She is packing up, must have been cut already. Bah. Wonder if she will wait to say bye or just leave. A little bit of me wants her to leave without a *'bye'*. Most of me doesn't, but that majority also knows the little chance I have of winning her from her burden of a situation at this time. I wish I didn't understand. That ignorance would allow for a little bit of hope. Maybe she will leave him for me, but like times before she is stuck with the precedent of the last five or so years. From my experience, barring a severe occurrence, it has been for the better duration of my interest.

I do my job for a little more, mostly bullshitting and staring at the clock waiting to leave. I can't see her. She must have left. Good. Now cut I tell everyone *'I'm leaving so they can run their own stupid food'*.

Wonder what my pseudo girlfriend is doing. I send her a feeler text assuming she will drop whatever she's doing to come hangout. She texts back and wants to hang out. Nicely done. I tell her to give me a little because I'm almost out of work.

"Hey!"

She didn't leave

"Oh hey!"

Well shit.

"What are you up to tonight?"

Already have plans.

"Letting you buy me a drink."
"Sounds about right. First one is me."

Bah. We get our first one for free. Tricky stupid jerk leave me alone. She is so awesome.

I text the other one some nonsense about something.

We get a couple rounds. Hanging out after work is fine because we work together. Anything else would be falooziп'. The time is predictably enjoyable. Coworkers smirk at us when they think I'm not looking. I'm not - just some great peripheral vision. It is too good. It really sucks. I wonder why she is doing this to me. My phone keeps buzzing in my pocket. It doesn't get answered.

"Well I should get going... I was supposed to be home a while ago." as cool as I can
"Yea I'm supposed to meet up with some people." beating me to the *hanging out with other people* part.
"Yea me too."

I walk her out to where we should make out. We don't. I should go in for it anyway, but then I might end the only connection I have to her. As much as I want to I would never be smart enough to do that. My testicles have shrunk up into my throat so it doesn't really matter. I gargle out a 'goodnight' and bend over to hug her. She hops in the car. She turns the engine on while giving me a last look and a wave. I return the gesture while letting a fart out of my ass I have been holding for too long. Her car is stopped at the red light in the direction I need to walk. I walk the other way and try not to shit myself. Once I know she is gone I turn around - there is nothing for me in the direction I was walking.

I feel spiteful now. I check the messages. There are three from her. One telling me where she is going. A second telling me she left and a last one telling me she is going home to bed. Nice. Tread water so long just to drown in the kiddie pool. I start texting her to stay out and blame everything on work. I should really stop doing this to myself. Pick a direction and stick to it.

I should go home.

I stand on a corner and light a cigarette. I waste a good 20 minutes standing, actually sitting since there is a bench I took advantage of about 19 minutes ago right beside me (now under me). There is probably some booze at home. I can drink myself stupid for what seems like free. No work tomorrow so I can sleep until the next day. I will be lonely. I will check what my landlord is doing. Meh. It will be worse in public. Everyone will be hammered already and it will be even lonelier until I catch up so quick I have to run home to throw up for the rest of the night. I want somewhere that is not here, out or home.

I smoke some more cigarettes and think of the penguin club. He seemed happy. All the distractions, drama and other nonsense didn't seem to pertain to him. I don't have that in me, although I'm still a faithful member by default. No credit to consciousness. I would benefit from ridding myself from everything. No headaches, confusion, insecurities - get it done and save up for next year, saving hair and healthy blood pressure.

Every morning I wake up with pits in my stomach, half the time not even shit related. Maybe I will get something out of it - most likely something awful and debilitating and terrible. What I should do is get real emo and drink myself to incoherency. That is a great idea.

I get home and b-line for the booze. I'm not sure exactly where it is so there is a bunch of mini b-lines. None in the fridge or cupboards, lunacy. A memory strikes of my landlord wobbling to bed with a bottle the other night.

There are some noises from his room. Music? TV? Not much thought escapes me as I swing the door open, confronted with him and some chick both really naked. She's on all fours. He is behind her. They both must be black out drunk. I make eye contact with both of them, but neither gives a look of *'get the fuck out of here'*. Both look concentrated and in some serious pain.

I continue to stand in the doorway as they go at it, forgetting that I am here as I scan the room for some booze. After looking left to right there is a bottle on the dresser right next to me, some of the world's finest. It must have been one of those *'wanna go watch something in my room blablabla'* things where you bring booze just in case you don't start screwin' around immediately - eventually thinking *'thank Christ I didn't drink any of that or I would be vomiting on her back right now'*.

I grab it and say thanks. She grunts and he says "you're welcome."

Back on the couch. This would be a great time to have my own place. I could go for some self-seduction right this second, really go at myself with a few diverse clips from multiple web sites making sure it is out to the last. Chasers are dry. Could not find anything but water. It is not ideal but the chlorine mixes well with the bleach of the booze.

There is five shots lined up in anything ranging from a shot glass (broken) to a dried out gourd my cousin brought back from Togo, Africa. They are used for water down there but I use them for decor and liquor. Ending the row is a glass of water. The first two are easy. The third and fourth, not so much. The fifth gets caught up in my throat and I hold back the vomit.

The drunk comes quickly. I'm talking to myself, asking a bunch of questions I don't know the answers to, or do and don't want to think about them along with lectures of how to be a better person. I bore myself and pour another shot. The floor is sticky. I'm not sure why. I take a swig straight from the bottle to get rid of the self-lectures and questions. The noise from the bedroom is dying now. I think they both may be dying slowly on top of each other. I can't wait 'til tomorrow when they come out and see me naked on the couch. I need to do something. Hopefully impressive so I would want to tell people, but not so impressive that people would stop listening right away because it's so sweet.

I wake up with boxers and some partial dignity - my junk fell out the dick flap, fully visible to those walking out the door. I hear her ask 'is he ok?' Of course I am mind your business. I didn't ask if my buddy was raping you last night so shut the hell up and enjoy the sight of my mangled penis.

After releasing her back into the wild he comes back in and sits on the couch. I tuck my junk back in to make it suitable man time.

He sighs 'holy hell what a night."
"That good eh?"
"No idea who that is."
"Good. Remember me joining for a bit?"
"What?"
"Not in a cool/disturbing way. Just stopped in to say hi and grab some booze."
"Oh yeah... Nope."
"I spit up vodka on the floor."
"Yeah I can feel it under my feet."
"I cleaned it up don't worry."
"Good."

The TV isn't on yet we both stare at the screen.

"I think I have problems." not moving my mouth.
"Drinking by yourself?" possibly concerned.
"No no no. That's fine." laughing. "Nothing like that. Girl stuff."
"You and what's-her-face?"
"Half. The other one from work too. Not sure who to go for."
"Yeah she wants you. AND she's hot."
"Fact. She is hot. But I am pretty sure I am in love with the one from work though."
"She is really hot too!"
"Fact. She is also hot."

"Problems."
"I figure it goes one of two ways... I hold out for her hoping she drops her dead beat boyfriend while losing the other who obviously wants me or I settle and she breaks up with her stupid boyfriend and sees that I am with someone else, ultimately forgetting I ever existed. I would then break off what I have to go and chase her somewhere without success."

"Whoever you like best... I dunno." losing interest quickly.
"Yeah I'll figure it out..." losing interest myself.

We sit and pretend to listen to each other - back and forth talking about different things with no response to the other's previous statement. It is nice being a guy. You can count on a guy to underplay/ignore a predicament that is bothering you. It is fun, interesting and completely unhelpful besides that it makes you realize it doesn't really matter.

It's a trendy little coffee shop with free refills. I stopped to get a 17 dollar notebook before I came - I decided to start writing this morning. I have been told I have a knack for it but it was always one of those things that brought a sentiment of "Yeah... ok... you go do that..." Not from anyone, just myself. Pessimism has its perks, none being a gift of ambition.

Not sure what to start about. I doodle in the margins leaving space for any potential words that might come to mind. The best I guess would be to write what I know - little bitch feelings and women who I love that will never love me. Yeah... ok... you go do that...

It's good that there are free refills. I am on my 4th or 5th cup now and I'm starting to get the shakes. It is raining outside. I like the rain. There's not enough hot hipster chicks here. Maybe I should write my story - take my mind off my current situation but conjure up old feelings. I should just combine the two - raw feelings work best I think. I would like to do something that solicits a genuine reaction, good or bad not related to someone's food being screwed up on my part. That will take some planning. No it won't. All I have to do is just start writing. It will come. I will worry about being good once I realize it sucks on the edit. People relate to it. There lives suck too. They will laugh and feel bad for me. I don't want them to, but they will even though they think I'm an ass hole for some reason. They will think there is something wrong with me. There won't be, but they will believe it either way. I have already lived it kinda so I should just go - better have an ending with my nose clenched in some hot chicks butt cheeks.

I start writing from the beginning, back when things were good, when I could look at a kid without thinking of mine floating around in my head, when I couldn't remember what what's-her-face's name was.

Around the time I figured out that I probably wouldn't ever figure out what is going on. An ignorance-is-bliss state with the acknowledgement of itself with little remorse or desire to fight it.

I write for hours, burning through pages while randomly going back and changing things. Besides these immediate changes, I probably won't read this until I'm done. That would be detrimental - I hate everything I do. I would give up before I give myself a chance at a chance. Thinking about it now I might just go get a beer.

At work once again, distracted as usual with the girls. I am slowly losing the one that likes me. She seems tired of my shit. My saucy co-worker still flirts with me here and there but I am making a conscious effort to stop. Never win a girl with attention anyway. Some of the girls are babbling to each other. Bored shitless I go over to eavesdrop.

"I bet you're happy" to me with a stupid smug look on her face.
"Bet I'm not." almost pissed she would think I could be happy about something.
"They broke up" still smug.

I open my mouth to say something before it registers. Fighting a smile my head dips, a little pissed that that did make me a little happy, a lot happy.

"What do you think of that?!" getting cocky now.

I smack the bread baskets out of her hands to the floor and head to the kitchen window.

I do not like people knowing stuff about me. In an ideal world it wouldn't matter, everything would work out. Things don't work out when everyone knows what is going on with you. Then you are doomed by questions about '*how it's going*' and smothering condolences. I'm already cursed with glances of pity from most of the people here knowing that I've liked her since the start.

What do I do now? Yeah I'm happy that's over with, at least momentarily. Common sense tells me it can't be over so quick and simple. I tell me that maybe it's been a long time coming. Experience chimes in, agreeing with common sense. Dr. Pessimism then diagnoses that I'm a piece of shit so it doesn't matter - take a vacation and forget about it - go get herpes from a foreigner or something. They're all hard points to swallow but it's entertaining having these conversations with myself.

I shouldn't try to hang out with her right away, but I have to strike before they get back together for the reason of *this is different.* If I text her now she will know I just found out - we secretly both know the other's work schedule. Why hasn't she said anything to me yet? She doesn't want to be desperate. She knows they will just get back together. She is in love with me and doesn't want to scare me off. I will never know as long as this dick of indecision is reamed so far up my ass.

I text her to hang out.
She agrees.
For the rest of the night customers think I'm delightful.

It is Wednesday evening and I'm driving to her place at school. We decided a week night would be best for a real date-ish sort of thing instead of a rushed uncomfortable drink after work. We didn't talk about it, that's what went through my head at the time. The drive is inconvenient but I would drive it a hundred times to see her once. I'm nervous. Never good. Stomach is churning around reminding itself that I haven't took a number three in a little bit.

I have one of those thermal shirts on that seem nice despite their cheapness. They seem nice to me but my style hasn't changed since I made the switch to jeans from sweat pants in 7th grade. I have one of those linen shirts but I think it's too wrinkly even for linen. My jeans are fresh from the drier even though I didn't wash them - have to get that junk-hugging going. My shoes are most likely out of date which may mean they are again in style, but I don't think I've lived long enough to span quite that range across the fashion spectrum. Taking my whole get up in, I wonder how I have ever attracted anyone but military recruiters.

TEXT: Where ya at?!

Oh nice, sign of interest and definite arousal.

Close. Whatcha doin?
Getting ready. What are you wearing?
Thong and socks you?
Shutup! So I know what to wear!
Oh. Waffle shirt jeans shoes
Waffle?... Oh ok thermal. gotcha.

I put the phone down and get off the rumble strips on the side of the highway. Should be an interesting night.

Coming up to her apartment I get her on the phone to see where I should park. She tells me she will just meet me outside the door because parking sucks. So much for my assumed quick sexual romp before dinner. I wait with the car in the middle of the street. She walks out of the doors looking for my car. She's really beautiful - a lot more so than me. I beep obnoxiously. She sees me and heads over. It seems like it's in slow motion but I think it's my heart beating unhealthily fast from the sight of her and the thousands of cigarettes I've loved in the past.

She gets to the door of my car and tries to open it. It's locked. I jostle around to unlock it like I'm in a friend's car and don't know where the lock thing is. I finally just reach over and do it pre-mid 90's style. She gets in and a wave of not-shitty-smelling air rushes in. I can't tell exactly what she's wearing, even with all my perfume experience. I do know it's what I imagine her sitting on my face would smell like - roses and glitter. Glitter would be more for the visual stimulation and roses because I don't have a favorite smell besides the essence of smoke-soaked clothes on my parents after a night out where I was waiting impatiently at home hugging a blanket my mom got me one time. That would be weird if that's what her sitting on my face would be - she doesn't smoke.

Out of my head and back into the car.

"Hey!" a child to his hot baby sitter.
"Hi..." out of breath for some reason. Maybe it's cold or something. I don't know I've been sweating for the last year or so.

I mistakenly go for the in-car hug leaving me open and vulnerable to an awkward greeting.

"So where we going?"
"I gotta place a friend told me about. A nice Jewish place."

I normally don't comment on these things but the friend that suggested threw that in there. Not being, to my knowledge, anti-jew I don't find a problem with it. She laughs.

"A nice Jewish place? Well then! Should have dressed up a little more." Mocking.
"Get out of the car." laughing thinking only if we get naked.

She pretends to get out, most likely thinking the same thing, but also like me too small-balled to go for it.

There's a grumble in my stomach.

Beautiful.

The place lives up to its possibly inappropriate introduction. It looks like what I now think is what a Jewish place looks like. After thinking for a second on its Jew-ness I laugh and recognize I would never have thought that without pre-exposure to the thought - *yeah that's super Jewish...* with the walls, bar, chairs and people and such.

She asks why I am laughing. I let her know my exact thought process with the background of where the Jewish thing came from in the first place. She gets a kick out of it, admitting she did the same thing. We laugh into the nice Jewish place. Once sat, there's a brief break followed by bursts of some more laughter on both parts. It takes a little for us both to settle completely.

It wasn't even that funny.

We order drinks as the waitress hands us menus. She gets a cosmo, or an equivalent similar drink with a funky name. Somehow caught off guard with the ordering process I order some light beer.
Disappointing but probably not bad in the long run - I can drink about a thousand of them and not even throw up.

Should be interesting.

The menu has something close to four thousand pages littered with inserts about specials and other nonsense I will stare at but never read. I *hmph* while barely getting through the title of the first section. She does something short of a giggle. I scan the endless list of items, occasionally reading a word or half a description. Before I realize it, the waitress is back impatient for our order.

"Um... I've read about five non-sequential words on this menu so far. I need more time."
"Yeah." laughing "I've just been looking at the border illustrations"

The waitress leaves in a huff. Laughing continues to be the theme of the evening. Between her obsession with the border pattern and me reading like an elephant, our waitress comes back a few times, none resulting in any order taken. We keep laughing. Finally, after much bullshitting, our waitress squeezes an order out of us. She gets the something-or-other while I breeze over the newspaper menu for something that won't make me look like a slob. I manage an order muddled with profanities. The waitress says something condescending and leaves. We laugh at ourselves.

The night is great. Better than the disaster I was prepping myself for. The conversation is free and flowing and without the need of any go-to topic starters. We only stop to feed ourselves, silent for a few extended moments, half the time talking anyway and laughing at the other's incoherency. Neither is polite - both barely keeping it together enough not to spit on the other.

The night is going too fast for me. Not between us, but rather the actual seeming duration. This is the first night that has been care free and fun. Even when I have been drinking with friends lately it has been for my own personal reasons. Now, dinner well gone, only heels of drinks are on the table. I want to order another round to extend the evening but I made the switch from light beer to a nice Belgian and I'm beginning to be completely smashed. Being the first real time spent together, I'm selfish in that I never want to let her go, especially not now. I want her for myself. Definitely cannot get another round or this mind babble will be pooing out of my mouth. She may be receptive of these words. I may be receptive to a punch in the face from myself if I let me actually believe that. These feelings are quickly filled with the ones about how every female I've met wants to have sex with me. Weird how the best emotions are a collaboration of a bunch of little terrible ones - anxious, nervousness, doubt. Not sure if those are actual feeling, but either way... I know they are adding up to something I've never felt without a certain level of convincing.

This is around the point where I would stop hanging out with a girl - when I think she's feeling the exact way I am not. Hope she's not like me. There's no way this can work out. I've shot this type of situation down too many times from the other side. Karma is a real thing and I'm a bit more than a bit overdue for some. I'm not pessimistic. I just know these sorta things don't work out for me.

I'm pessimistic.

This is different. I can feel it. God I sound like a high school girl. Why don't I just see how it pans out. Let go and have fun. That's when it gets entertaining mostly because I can derive hilarity from the oncoming disappointment. I may have some problems.

I get back from my mental break down as we are pulling up to her place. That was beneficial - good to know that on top of being drunk, I was completely somewhere else while driving back. It would be nice if I could turn off my thinking thing like normal people do when they drink. But no, drinking embellishes every thought streaking through my brain.

Ok stop it.
Let go.
This isn't the defining moment of our whatever-the-hell together.
Have fun and enjoy this you stupid ass.
Ok.
Good plan.
Ready.
Go.

I come back once again but now in her apartment. I wish I knew this trick in college. Usually I could talk my way out of going home with any willing participant. Wonder what I did. Probably a movie or something - she's routing through her collection of four.

"It's in here somewhere!" looking for something in particular.
"Good." walking around looking.

There's no real living room - at least no room with a couch. An awkward bed laying is in store for what I'm assuming is going to be a movie watching session.

"Got it." holding up a beat up copy of *So I Married an Axe Murderer*. I like that movie. Haven't seen it in a while either. Hurray. In her room she plops it in her computer (one of those 27 inch iMac thing) and flops down sideways across the bed on her stomach. Her position is less than ideal but I could be more pissed about many other things. I'm not expecting her to spread her legs and yell *'come and get'r'* – actually I prefer she never does that.

I take a moment to think for a minute about strategy. Body position is key, the key, the only thing I need worry myself with here. Too far and I am a sexless coward. Too close and I am a forward pervert that should've handed her the money for dinner and asked if she would swallow if I tipped her and smacked her ass in such a way. As I run these ideas through my head I get bored and roll down next to her, fibers throughout pop and tear audibly, nudging a bit on the over-roll but back on myself for the landing.

"Hey now!" without looking over.
"Well hey..." thinking stuff.

I like the movie, not that I'm watching it. I only know this because I've seen it before at an inappropriate age. She's playing tough - not looking at me after funny parts or returning my ankle jabs to her feet. She's being stupid. I like it. She must have done her homework, or genuinely disinterested. Either way I'm going to bruise the shit out of her ankles if I have to.

Well, I'm slowly becoming exhausted. Mike Myers is now running from Harriot in the hotel suite. My elbows hurt too much for continued use. Shoulders are rendered useless when lying flat. My ankles I think are bleeding and my neck has a kink in it from staring somewhere between the computer and her face.

Oh shit its Ruth. No way.

Still on her elbows, unfazed and relentless like a stubborn mule that only does things to do them...

"Fuck it..."

The axe flies between Mike's legs as I grab and push her near shoulder over opposite, pinning both her wrists out wide. She squeaks out something I don't care to understand before I begin swallowing her face. Her arms go taught against mine. Not sure if she's going for my back or a phone to ring in a sexual assault I let her hands free and continue eating her face. Her one arm wraps around my waist, the other around my neck. I think *'sweet'* for a sec before remembering I have no strength left in my arms or shoulders. I'm shaking noticeably. I shift all energy to one arm, letting the other collapse, rolling us over to a vice-versa position. Thank graciousness because I was ready to fall on top of her, most likely crushing her to the near inconvenience of a struggling breath. My hands are on her hips holding firm but gentle in some void of natural physics. My abs have been stretching since we first laid down so they are ready to give a little back to the situation. I sit up and start chewing on anything my mouth touches - neck, shoulder, arm, tit, side boob, cheek, chin - nothing is safe from a potential mark of love. Her clothes taste like cotton and are making my mouth dry so I rub my hands up under her shirt. She stops for a second and laughs, pushing her shirt back down. I hesitate with her and stare like a confused dog - head cocked with tongue out and everything.

"No it's fine..." going at the shirt again.
"Oh is it now?" laughing and showing either signs of submission or acknowledgment that I'm not going to give up anytime soon - same difference in my mental notebook.

My struggles persist but are slowly paying off with my assurance that *'It's fine'* and *'I wouldn't worry about it'*. It's almost a game at this point. Laughing like gays, we wrestle around battling for shirt position. One moment I manage to get it off one of her arms. A flash of her left boob blinds me for a bit. I regain whatever I lost only to find her shirt is completely back on with her smiling face above it. I can feel my face reflecting hers. It's pretty bad because the smile muscles in the back of my head are cramping - shocked at the level at which they must perform right now. The position of the second having her on top of me again, I sit up, hands accompanying to the back of her head, and kiss her like a working woman (loins-for-hire) can only imagine. Both bodies relax, even my abs - half from the moment and half from exhaustion - as we roll over to our sides - my left, her right.

I forget about stripping her naked and enjoy the moment, knowing it'll be over quicker than I'd prefer. I look down to take it all in and realize we are both mostly naked. Apparently my subconscious is stuck on autopilot and never rests.

Well, here I am again. Another naked (mostly) girl lying next to my confusingly successful body. How did I get here? Usually I don't have to go back too far - leave the bar with an *'oh hi'* and back to present. Predictably, this time it's different. It's past the previous couple hours, way past - not days, not weeks. Usually people are excited when they reach their goal. Not to say women are meant to be goals, but when you want something and are willing to strive for it, there's not much difference in this area. I've been after her for so long that right now seems like a dream, but this isn't what I was going for. Am I completely and utterly aroused right now? Yes. On a scale from 1 to 10, I feel like a little boy watching his first porno all over again, but this isn't what I was going for. This isn't home plate. I'm not going to lie, I've had this before and it always ends up in the shitter - feelings feeling like shit.

I want more now. I don't want another fizzling fling to reminisce on, or more likely feel bad about. I'm done... finished... out...

I roll onto my back solo for a second, then pull her over so she's half laying on me with her head sideways flat on my chest. I take some deep breaths, ironically bobbing her head up and down a couple times until she pokes up and looks at me.

"Well you got quiet all of a sudden" her chin digging into my chest deeper with every word.
"I hope you know this isn't the reason I've been after you for so long..."
"Well I hope not..."

It's the next morning and I'm up early. Last night went well and I've been having to think of terrible things in order to give my smile muscles a little bit of a break - dead babies, childhood diseases/disorders, parents dying and anything else that would tug at the heart of the tin man. I'm drinking coffee and cleaning, blasting Annie Lenox's 'Walking on Broken Glass'. It's sunny and I'm wearing sunglasses inside. All the windows are open, letting the breeze stride through with the wisp of my emotions fluttering alongside. Looks like everything is working out.
I act like a young idiot for some time today.

It's been two weeks since everything started 'working out' for me. Life's gone quite to shit since. Above a stray one word text response, Jen and I haven't conversed. Something is even more rotten in my rotten worthless shit of a life. What used to be fun, enjoyable banter between us is now a strenuous effort to get some confirmation that she still knows I'm alive.... and just when I had it all perfect - excited to settle down and one of the few men that's happy not to be fucking everything in sight.

I should've known something was amiss when things started making me happy. The only girl I've wanted in some time? And not for her ass and tits?! Why would that ever work out for me?! I should've tried to sleep with her.

I want this to be different...

What a stupid thing for me to think. Different from what? Different from having mediocre to awesome sex right away and then having that girl fall in love with me immediately? Yeah... That would've been awful considering that's all I really wanted - her to fall in love with me. No. I had to go about it differently. Stray from what I know at the perfectly wrong time. Why wouldn't I change things up now? I'm a changed man who know what he wants. Apparently I want things to be like they were when I didn't want them that way. Perfect timing you stupid asshole. I should've slept with her. At least then I could say I had her for one night. For one night we were in love... things just didn't work out. I could've blamed it on just about anything - timing, distance, her boyfriend that she is undoubtedly back together with right now.

Nope. I wanted to play it unfamiliarly. I wanted to go off the reservation and do it my own way - my new own way thinking that my 'old self' is gone, forgotten and dumb. However, my old self is just laughing and not saying, but yelling 'YOU STUPID FUCKING MORON!! WHY?!" My response being *'I know... definitely not an intelligent move on my part'*. I zone in and out of all the *'what ifs'* and *'motherfuckers'*, drinking aggressively in between and during.

What the hell am I going to do?!

I've ran this question through my head too many times. Not once has it been answered. I posed some possibilities, but nothing really sticks. One was to start sleeping with everyone until I contract a life-threatening disease. It's an unattractive option at best and would take some time to get one of the real bad ones. Other possibilities are a little more realistic, but truth to fact I'm really just indifferent to everything right now. I don't have feelings to go out and get some, but if it were to fall on my lap it would be whatever, probably thinking *'Yeah, sure, now ya do it you stupid shit'*, digging me deeper into the outhouse's refuge of my life.

Hmmm.

I mill about the house with tons of self-pity. There's a lot of plopping going on, putting things down loudly - beers, packs of cigarettes, books I pick up and realize I don't want to read, myself. That'll show the powers that surround me. If they have ears they will be mildly irritated. I'm sitting on the couch like a kid who wants to leave wherever he is against his will - legs slutty wide, arms out to my sides, palms up, back on the edge of the couch and my head at an angle of the possessed.

I wish there was someone here to yell at me for any of the things I'm doing so I could get pissed at something else. The TV has an annoying glare on it. Stupid TV. I'm tired and restless, a terrible combination for any sort of mood. I pull my shorts up and stare at my gleamers. They are white - pasty white. God I'm gross. No wonder I suck. I'm in California and I look like paper.

I hate this.

I hate myself.

I've completely stopped trying to get in contact with her. I don't like being ignored or blown off, figuratively (and actually literally - I find it uncomfortable and struggle with most efforts). I wish I never see her, but work makes it difficult. We work together every so often. I don't go up to the hostess stand though. I stay in my hole downstairs hoping she doesn't come to say hi. On some occurrences she has to piss - back of my mind hoping she's pretending, front of mind thinking emergency diarrhea. Whether it be either, I just say hi and stick my fat head back in the kitchen window. She doesn't break stride - back of my mind thinking *'she doesn't play into these games'*, front of my mind thinking *'get over yourself...and her'*. I make like I have a poo poo coming on and am not there when she's done pretending to piss. I hate her like fried food.

Work is slow. I'm irritable and short-fused in all aspects; customers, co-workers and myself - thinking in circles about how she really likes me with complete doubt sickling the cycle once every go-around.

"She does because... She does because... She does because..."
"Nope she doesn't."
"She does because... She does because... She does because..."
"Nope, still no you pathetic asshole."

Standing in the back hallway, I'm facing five inches from the wall, completely zoned out with my head visibly circling. A crack or some sorta sound kicks me out of it. It's one of the sultry waitresses. I don't say anything and turn back to my buddy the wall. She walks by...

"Sorry"
"For what?" confused but not.
"Oh... You don't know?"
"I can probably guess, but what?"
"She's back with him"
"Hmm..."

She continues by me. I feel like I was just told that I have herpes after avoiding confirmation even after the appearances. An if-I-don't-know-I-don't-have-it sorta thing. Great. My suspicions confirmed. The back of my mind is full of shit. I go through the motions for another set time until it hits ten. I tell everyone I'm leaving, or at least yell it around them - not caring if they hear or not. I grab my shit, knowing that there's more somewhere else in the building. It's not important now. She's not up front.

Shit.

I can't leave without giving her a brief, impersonal goodbye with no stoppage. That'll show her good-like. Scanning the bar and other areas I can't find her. That bitch. She beat me to it. She left without a bye. Hardball she wants, hardball she gets.

I fuck it and head to the door, grumbling to myself while ignoring everyone that probably isn't paying attention to me in the first place. Verging on escape, I see her. My heart lays a dump down to my stomach and I almost vomit directly on her. She smiles...

"Hey." like the evil bitch she is
"Hey. What are you up to?" frozen like the ball-less ass I am.
"Just going home to hang out with the parents." like the evil bitch she is
"Oh that's nice. See you later." Wondering why she even asked me what the fuck I was doing anyway

I leave the bar, almost in a run. I'm out of breath - half from the quasi run and half from talking to her off guard. I don't know where I'm going, but I know I'm going somewhere. Tonight's not the night to go home and sleep it off. I'm going out and getting inappropriate. On the hunt I'm going to find a girl tonight. At first I'll give half a shit what she looks like. After the liquor and booze I'm about to drink increases, the quality of necessary outward appearance will most likely decrease. I don't care. Time to get at the town like I never have before. This place hasn't even experienced half of what they should have by now.

I'm drunk off aspiration and oxygen deprivation from thinking of such. I may not even need but a drink or two, as long as they're doubles. Even if I only need a few, I'll drink a ton. Tomorrow I will regret everything I'm about to do and it will be the biggest of slaps in her face. Not quite close, or even possible, but it'll seem so to me. Maybe her and her parents will be out and about - nothing like impressing the parents with a good jag and whiffs of whiskey filling the air around you. If there's one thing I learned from college it's that absolutely everyone is impressed with a drunk monkey.

I text churchy my plans and inform him he should join. I haven't really hung out or even spoke with him lately because of my lame depression, a depression I swore I would never allow myself again.

However, I did promise to make something of myself too. Look how that turned out so far.

The closest bar is within a block or three. I'm not exactly sure of the distance, but I know where it is kinda so I should be good.

There's another bar on the way that passed by my mind. Might as well make a bar crawl out of it.

It's a dive, one of my favorites since I've been here. I don't talk about it much. It's more of a local hang out, neighborhood sorta thing. I've become a regular of sorts so I get nods from the regulars as I walk in. There's very little eye contact, probably because of the obvious mood I'm in, most likely because they're all drunks who really don't give a shit. I don't blame them. They'd probably care less if I shared what was going on right now. I know I would do the same. Another guy with girl problems - boo hoo. Half are probably divorced and the other virgins. No room for complaints on my part now. The bartender throws a PBR down.

"Thanks... and a shot of Jameson please?"
"One of those nights?"

He knows I work at the bar down the street and attributes my aura to that. I don't blame him. Why would I? Stupid thing to say.

I swing back the red white and blue, then the shot, followed by some more patronage like a sandwich digesting in a homeless drunk's stomach.

I feel no taste. It's similar to water right now. I immediately order another shot and suggest I may need another bald eagle-delivered beer.

It's one of those nights.

There's a girl across the U-shaped bar. Lighter hair, maybe blond. I can't tell, it's a little dark. I stare at her until she happens to scan the bar through me. I smile and give a discretely obvious wave. She pauses for a moment long enough for me to know she noticed and then continues, obvious to me she doesn't approve. I laugh and order two more whatever the hells. The booze sandwiches are coming and going quick like a high teenager through bags of anything he can get his hands on. Dried prunes? Why not?

There's little to no prospects here accepting of my bullshit. I can tell because no one is talking to me yet. One more shot and I ask for my tab.

57 dollars. Shit, like fucking gambling - 20 minutes and nothing but debt to show for it. Well, give me about a half hour and I can probably conjure up something, especially at the pace I'm going.

I tip 30 dollars because that will make me feel better

I don't feel any better and I leave.

There's a buzzing in my pants. I haven't been horny in so long I consider it to be that. It's not, just my phone, although it may have gotten me going just now. It's churchy. He's going to meet me at the next bar.

Hurrayyyy.

I talk to myself in a muffled mumble while I keep it together for the walking duration. I'm already talking to myself.

It's one of those nights.

The buildings around me are unfitting for where I should be going. It makes sense though because I'm not going the right way. A simple mistake that could have happened to anyone, I turned left instead of right. I turn around hoping I'm going the right way, second guessing myself for what I assume is going to be the next few months.

Someone is smoking a cigarette on a porch step. I remember how much I love cigarettes, how much I need one right this second. Maybe I should ask for one. Maybe I should offer some money. No one actually takes any money offered. Done. I'm doing it. I walk up to what looks like a dude confidently and almost trip over the smooth, level sidewalk.

"Hey... I'll give you like... 2 bucks for a cigarette." undoubtedly wavering.
"Ok" excited for money.

Motherfucker. I give him 2 bucks, not too pissed because after all, I got a cigarette. Dollar bills are worthless anyway. They're like pennies for assholes like me. I usually spend every one I have on a jukebox song, just as much of a waste unless some girl loves the pick knowing it was you. Music is a wonderful thing, as long as it results in getting laid one way or another. Other than that it's just noise.

"Do I get a light for my money?" dead serious because I don't have one.

He laughs and chucks me his lighter. After faltering for a second or 3 I manage, say thanks and head on my way, completely forgetting I just gave a bum 2 bucks for a cigarette, a fucking menthol.

A few minutes pass as I'm in tobacco limbo dreaming of better things, along with complete randomness - how it would feel if my face was the bottom of my shoe. Rubbing my face from my imagined pain I hear my name shouted a short distance away. By this point I've forgotten exactly what I'm doing. Confused to who would be screaming my name right now I twirl like an ugly princess with a tobacco habit. Smoke gets in my eyes. Temporarily blinded I scream a response of *'please come get me'* like a blind man searching for Jesus in Jesus times. Water is rushing from my eyes, maybe wine? Like that wedding thing? More likely Jameson and America's piss. I wish - licking my tears would be a whole bunch better.

Wiping the miracle from my eyes I hear some laughter coming closer. The local gang of leper-bothering kids? Hope not. If it is, I'm in luck. I don't have leprosy. The laughing is now all around me and I start getting pushed around. I try and look but I'm blinded by Jameson. Damn kids. Can't they see that I can't? Jerks.

Then, assumedly by the black magic I've been practicing in the back hallway at work, I'm weightless and ascend into the air. I'm flying. This is all a dream? My life doesn't suck and I'm not drinking myself into a forgettable stupor? God, life, my dream, is good.

As I'm floating around in my dream, that feeling turns into that of a free fall. Skydiving now maybe? Nope. I hit something similar to the sidewalk I was just using. I come to out of my self-convinced dream and realize just dropped about 4 feet to the ground. The people laughing are my friends. Friends don't do this sorta thing you may say. Well, they do. I rub my face from the real pain across it. I'm all scraped up and probably bleeding somewhere. This fits perfect with how I was previously feeling, drunk. I can always blame my despondence on getting the shit kicked out of me for the rest of the night. Bartenders are more sympathetic towards the victims of minority muggings. The pain in my head, as well as all the other dense parts of my body, fill the empty pit I've had since leaving work.

"Come on" they all say as they leave me laying on the sidewalk "Let's drink!"
"Comin..." thinking *'eventually'* to myself.

Right now I can't pinpoint my exact body position so I roll around until my ass lands on the curb. Bringing my knees to my chest, one foot on the street, the other on the drainage thing, I see my still lit cigarette. I pick it up and take a puff, trying to forget not what just happened, but rather about the AIDS that are probably stuck to it. *'AIDS is dead'* I tell myself.

"That's disgusting" an attractive voice says in an everyday tone right behind me.

"I know..." turning to look "Oh... it's you!"

It's what's-her-face that I was talking to for a bit before that crazy she-devil ruined my life. I can't remember her name. I'll blame it on the drunk drop. It shouldn't be an issue anyway - we've known each other long enough that she won't notice I'm not saying her name, but not long enough for permanent residence in my memory.
"Yeah it's me."
"Sorry for not calling." half sorry, half drunk and horny (maybe my phone is vibrating again)
"You're an asshole"
"I know" sincerely "I'm a child that never knows what he wants, or how to go about doing things."
"You're an asshole"
"Fact. I am an asshole.... Buy you a drink?"
"You're drunk."
"YOU'RE drunk. I just got dropped on my head!" both possibly true, one for sure. I think I may give up lying, not that I ever really lied to begin with.
"Oh yeah... Sorry about that"
"You told them to do that didn't you..." saying this before realizing it's probably true.
"Nooooo" looking down like a dog that just shit in the living room
"Hmmmm" not caring to think of something real to say.
"They weren't supposed to drop you like that!" defending something she apparently didn't do.
"So you did tell them to do that"
"Maaaaayyybbbeeeeeeee" looking cute and to me in my drunkenly dropped state, vulnerable.
"Help me up and I won't hate you..."
"Shutup! I should hate you!" helping me up from my homeless bum position.
"Why?!" with a chuckle

She stops helping me up and lets me fall, no malice, just a sense of *'I think I'm in love with you'*. I laugh, not because of the situation, but rather the familiarity of it. No time like the present.

I get up with a fresh sense of *'it doesn't feel like I just got dropped on concrete'* and strut quickly up behind her. I kick at her heel, knocking it into her other ankle making her trip a little. She stops.

"I'm going to kill you..."
"I loooooveeee you too..."

And with this I head into the bar, most likely starting something I'll regret tomorrow, just because it feels good tonight. This can only end in more apologies from me for neglect.

In advance, I'm sorry.

I really am.

The next morning comes a little quicker than the others. Making it a point to forget everything you're going through will do that to you I guess. Before I open my eyes I play the game of guessing where I am. The last clear thing I remember is being thrown in the air by my asshole friends. Then... walking in with what's her face after a brief back-and-forth, pseudo-apology session. My friends may have felt a little bad, or been acting in a regular way, because they ordered round after round shots I might have liked. Those shots are the last of what I remember close to clear. Them, and that girl invading my blurry personal space.

Eyes still closed I get a sense of my immediate location with my body sensors - back, shoulders, forehead. Partitions in the cushions say I'm on a couch. I jam my head into the crevice of the recently discovered furniture. It's rough, corduroy or something stupid like that. I'm developing brush burns, but it doesn't stop me because the pressure from the coarse cushions is alleviating the irritation from the knife I must have sniffed up my nose last night. Is my (churchy's) couch corduroy? In the last however long I've been out here I've never taken notice. Maybe it's the small ridged type of corduroy that almost seems like something better. Is this my couch bed I've been sleeping on?

Now I'm to the point of acknowledging that I may just be home. My shortcomings as a moral individual have fallen short for the first time that I'm willing to remember. Wary of licking the couch for the third of my sense tests, I attempt to open my eyes that are crusted shut with eye diarrhea and confusion. They manage to pry themselves open, leaving behind what could be the remnants of a toddler snotty runny nose. I'm blind and begin to panic for a second before realizing my head is still shoved deep between the couch cushions. I laugh, pull out and laugh again.

The place is unfamiliar but well decorated. I'm in a girl's house, just not her bed. There's potted plants aligned in a row, all still alive and not pot plants. There's a color scheme that makes sense. Things on the walls are framed and unwrinkled. A hint of girl flows by with the breeze from a curtained window. I'm on venus.

I figure, barring the likely chance I just wandered in here in the middle of the night and passed out, I'm welcome here to some extent since I was allowed to crash on the couch. Sitting up I wonder if she has a kitchen. Standing up I wonder to what extent can drinking yourself stupid really reach. I'm neither surprised nor disappointed when my wanderings come across a kitchen, neat and tidy with a closed dishwasher and decor not meant for practical use. The fridge seems promising with its magnets instead of tape and family photos instead of half-naked men labeled with the names of friends and myself.

The pictures catch my attention. I stand there, fridge half gaping, as I scan over the collage of images of places I've never been - not that I want to go to any, it's like regular cities you always hear of but never have any desire to go to, or at least I think so because there isn't a huge sphinx-lookin' thing in any of them. It's definitely the girl from my thought-to-be regrettable situation sprouting last night. She's hot. I think I always noticed that, but I can never be sure. Yes. She's hot. Noted.

Water...water...waterr....waterrrrr..wwwaaatttterrrrrrrrr......

There it is. Big jug of water right in the middle, right in front of my face.

"Goodmorning..." a cute voice radiates from somewhere besides the inside of the fridge

----

Grabbing a jug of water out of the fridge my head swings towards the voice as I prepare for my finest greatings - well hello. It's whats-her-face, not surprising. I move my mouth assuming my voice would characteristically follow. Instead of a *'well hello'*, a dried gargle of nonsense sifts out of the back of my throat. She gives a predictable face like *'really?'*. In my head I answer *'yes really'* as I begin to open every cupboard she has.

"The glasses are in the one on the end... You can use the green ones if ya want"

I give a thumbs up not wanting to try the talking thing again until I get some liquid back in that dry vagina of a throat that's going on right now. Smiling like a mute I go over to the cabinet she pointed toward. There's a bunch of colors and I pull out a blue one. I hear her *'hmph'* - probably because my glass isn't red. I'm not for much caring at this point so I don't hesitate to fill the glass and chug its contents.

My first gulp is too big, briefly realizing why girls prefer not to do such things right before I start choking and spitting up in the sink. My eyes start to water accompanied with sweat and snot. I can feel her disappointment engulfing me as I continue to dry heave/cough. Maybe I should ask if she wants to go do it, or maybe if we did it last night would be a launch spot. The water helps. Speaking is half back.

"Well hello" wiping away the array of mucosa layering my face like the amniotic sac I would've been better off never escaping - all with a smile.

I feel like shit by the way.

"You owe me!" shaking her head with some indecisive smile. She's not mad - not sure what she is, but it's not mad.
"What? We do anal or something?!"
"You ass..."
"Because I do owe you in that case... heard it's painful" interrupting before my comments convince her to get mad. "How 'bout breakfast?"
"It's noon"
"Great! Lunch!"
"..." moving stuff around without a purpose.
"Done. Let's go. I'm starving."
"Fine... Let me get changed..." with the enthusiasm of your hungover uncle after you have been begging him to play Connect Four with you since he woke up.

Well, I couldn't have done anything too terribly awful. I'm guessing I got sloppy drunk, hit on everyone, then invited myself to her house. 'But nothing's going on' she most likely told me. 'I wouldn't worry about it' is what probably followed by me. She then definitely sighed deeply with frustration and pre-regret. She could've told me to go fuck myself. I would've gone and tried for a bit until realizing I was in no shape and that I was on the couch in the living room.

She comes back out after a couple minutes.

Nika!!! I just remember her name (in the story and actually because I really forgot this whole time.)

She's dressed in a simple yellow cotton sundress. Her hair is thrown up askew from care, the way I like it. Couple buck sandals are slipped on her feet, a dark shade of some color I don't know the name of.

"Ready." as she leans over the kitchen table to grab her keys.

The cotton lays over her butt, stabbing my manhood with a crippling pleasure, not even touching. Me saying nothing she repeats:

"Ready?!" noticing my shift in physical feeling. She knows what she's doing, that bitch, and I love it.
"Yes mam"

It takes me about the length of the walk to the car to settle down to an appropriate state of arousal. She doesn't look at me but once on the way... and I'm pretty sure she's just looking both ways before she crosses the street - in the way of her lookin' out for stuff that may be detrimental to her well-being. I wonder how long whatever this is is going to last. Probably until I sober up in an hour and make a conscious decision while leaving wherever we're going to be to disconnect myself again. She's aware of this. That's why she's just looking for cars. Don't blame her - suppose I am too.

In her car we make small talk.... I make small talk - mostly about the music that's on and on the cleanliness of her car. I don't think she really cares about what I'm saying. I know I don't care. She looks really confused. I don't think I am as to why. She's not biting on any of my small talk so I guess I'll just shut up. I start whistling without realizing it.

"You are like a little child..." she says with a straight face.
"Like... a child with promise that just isn't challenged by the adults around him?"
"No... an untalented, A.D.D. ridden child that will get heavy into drugs before he gets to high school" Like this actually happened.
"It's not my fault I rock out"

She laughs reluctantly trying to stop as soon as she can. This is impossible when something really strikes you as funny. Unfortunately for her she finds me funny.

"Stop it!! You're not funny!!"
"Oh... just picturing me naked again then??"
"You're an ass..."

She rolls her tongue inside her mouth and finally looks over at me.

"You know that?! You're such an ass!!"

Of course I know this. I've been using it to my full advantage since I found the fine line between an ass and an asshole. They like asses. Girls don't like assholes and there is a faint line between the two:

Asses joke and make fun of things girls can control, like slightly tripping over nothing or mispronouncing a simple word. Assholes criticize girls' insecurities like looks and general life well-being. Asses hold doors open and tell the girl stuff like 'I'm never doing this for you again'. Assholes swing doors open, walk through and assume it will hang open long enough for the girl to follow. Asses mostly make fun of themselves because they don't want to hurt anyone's feelings kinda. Assholes only make fun of other people because they are assholes.

I'm an ass once again. Well, I guess just once starting at the beginning. It happens sometimes. The last paragraph is half bullshit because there's a lot of girls that like true assholes. Often times they have some sort of problem though. I don't know it by any other name than 'I-can't-get-those-girls-because-I-refuse-to-treat-them-like-true-shit-itus'

At least I'm day dreaming about this stuff now and not making noises or stupid comments about stupid stuff.

Is there ever going to be a time when I know what I'm doing?

Probably not. I know what I'm not doing - anything close to productive. I'm wasting a lot of time for multiple people including myself - mostly myself. It's only a night here and there for the people I hang out with.

What's the draw of me?

Why does anyone tolerate me?

Put me with anyone for a long enough period of time I will unknowingly say something offensive about something/someone they feel strongly about. Especially if the 'best band ever' topic comes up seeing that the Beatles suck and the stones aren't much better. And I wonder why I roll around most nights with a racing heart drenched in a cold sweat.

Epiphany.

I hate myself.

I think I may have said that earlier.

I think I was drunk at the time.

If you didn't know, I'm sorry.

I probably didn't know either.

I never know what to get when I go out to eat. It's not unlike at dinner, which I think I described before. I cruise over the options without reading any of them. It's really bad at diners like these that don't have any pictures on the menu. If they really wanted to make money they would have one picture of their most expensive meal. I would pretend to weigh my options, knowing that when the waitress comes I'm going to give a grumbled mumble and end up just pointing at the picture breathing out *'That...'* and *'yeah that's fine'* to whatever side she says, even if there's multiple to pick from. I'm never disappointed because food usually comes out. I'll eat anything when I'm hungry, as long as it's smothered in some sort of gravy-like ranch saucy stuff. If it isn't, I just drink water after every bite.

"Are you ready to order?" uncaring and impatient
"Yes I'll have eggs over easy and toast please" Nika(?) says.
"And you?" Looking at me
"I'll have that" pointing at something with a red star next to it.
"Bacon or sausage?"
"That's fine..."
"....?"
"Oh... the second one"

All the women laugh at me. I join in because what else am I going to do? Nika gives me the look of three, saying without speaking *'What the hell's wrong with you?...'* *'How do you get through life?...'* and *'Why am I here'.*

"Not sure" looking down and now reading the menu the waitress forgot to pick up.

She looks around wondering who I'm talking to. She shakes her head again, that is, if she shook it before. I can't remember and can only assume she did. I laugh wondering what she was expecting. She continues shaking her head for the first or second time. I join because I'm easily impressed. She stops shaking her head. I continue, now confused as to why I'm shaking my head and laugh as a result. I'm now shaking my head and laughing even harder while she just stares with a look of terrible awe.

"So what are we doing?... What are you thinking?"
"About what?" half serious, half joking because I know she'll be delightfully pissed, still laughing and shaking my head.
"Errrr... you're such an idiot."
"Thanks... yeah I know.... Um I don't know."
"Is this just another flingy-fun thing for you?"
"No... I never end up having fun with the flingy things... Well... actually they are fun until they aren't flingy things anymore."
"So what are you doing now then?"
"I dunno."
"Will this ever be more than you not having anything else to do?"
"I guess that depends if I ever find anything else to do - I don't really look much"
"God you're an ass!"
"Yeah I know... I'm sorry... I actually am..."
"So I should just not talk to you then?!"
"Probably not if it will make you feel better."
"How can you just say stuff like that?!"
"Like what?"

"Exactly what you're thinking."
"I would have to try and think something else to avoid it... and in that case I would still be saying exactly what I'm thinking."

She gives me a frustrated laugh and shakes her head.

"There are no words for you."
"Besides 'such an ass'?"
"Well of course."
"I'd like to be friends I think."
"You think?"
"Had to've or I wouldn't've been able to tell you." Bludgeoning to death the joke that wasn't funny to cover my inability to commit to any statement that escapes my anti-girl-liking-brain-filtered mouth.
"My god..."

I lean back and laugh like I'm too fat to see my own penis. She laughs too, but in a really hot way - leading into the span where I regret breaking this whatever off because I didn't get a chance to touch myself this morning and am still a bit sexy-touch deprived. Honestly I don't know what she really thought was going on. If she really wanted some leverage that may have actually possibly worked she would've slept with me to make me feel bad for doing so. She didn't even have to actually humor my pathetic penis, which I can unfortunately see. She could've just let me pass out in her bed, stripped me naked and glued my dick to the side of my leg. I might've stopped by the discount wedding ring shop if I woke up next to her butt with my junk just firmly adhered to my thigh. Instead I wake up on the couch with my face jammed in a crevice where only loose change and butt gas reside.

If she only gave it a moment's thought.

Buuuuuttttttttttttttttttttttt she didn't.

The rest of the meal goes splendid. She mostly asks me about stuff I said and if I meant what I said and blablabla. I can't remember most of what she does but I'm familiar enough with myself to know what I was thinking at the time:

Whaat arya doooin?   --- I want to have sex with you right now
Well that's stupid.   --- You should be having sex with me right now
I gotta shit   --- I'm going to diarrhea myself if I don't sit on
a toilet right now

She gets a kick out of this and the other shit we bullshit about. I have fun. I'm sure she does too, reluctantly. Food is all eaten or not good or ignored or something else. We get the check and I grab it. She insists on doing something about it but I just hold it up high and start yelling stuff incoherently while imitating her voice with a shrill scream and holding on a conversation with myself being both of us. She laughs and gets frustrated that I'm taller than her and she can't reach the check. When we get to the pay place she tells the check out lady person to let her pay for some of it. I tell that same check out lady person that she is my adopted nephew that suffers from ass burgers. That check out lady person, who is probably finishing up a triple shift that started last week, takes my card with no acknowledgement of either of us and hands me back the receipt to sign.

"Thanks for being so understanding" I say while I pet Nikka on the head.

She swats my hand away and hits me in the gut hard enough to worry me about voiding my bowels right there. She smiles, tells the indifferent lady thanks and walks out while I half stand next to the now texting check out lady . I say thank you, grab a mint and walk out behind the one I came with.

"Where ya goin?" --- I kinda liked it just then when you punched me and might now be regretting the back-and-forth we just had about not having sexy back-and-forths anymore.

I'm back on my couch - Churchy's couch. The TV isn't on, but I'm staring at it anyway. Nothing's on except stuff that will annoy me, but I don't want to be by myself right now and the TV is company even when off. I can turn it on whenever I feel like it, whenever I feel like zoning out to animals doing stuff. I'm so restless I can't even be restless. I look into the other room, imagine walking through it with no reward and mentally sit back down with myself. I come and go. I don't blame me. I'm horrible company right now. I stare at the ceiling and wonder what it tastes like. I stare a little more intently to try and make myself levitate to lick it. The farthest I get from the couch is when a let a rumbling blast escape my ass. I taste that, but not the ceiling. It makes me laugh. I laugh that I'm laughing at that. I pick up the remote and my wandering mental image of myself scans the mental channels, gets frustrated and turns the shit off again.

Work is a bunch times worse now. The lull in activity for half the night lets me think too much about everything. In the beginning of the night all the shitty things are by themselves to a degree. Of course then I start dwelling on one - maybe the job thing, or the girl thing, or the money thing, or the house thing, or the everything. The everything would be a combination of all the other things. One leads into the other into the other which leads back to what might've been the first. Doesn't matter if it was the first or not... it's just leading into the next thing anyway just biding time till it circles round and jams right up its ass again.

A ticket comes up and the cook lays down the food with a joke I don't listen to. I read the ticket to see where it's going as he realizes I'm not in the lightest of moods.

"Ya ok man?" as severely sincere a kitchen guy can be.
"Nope" avoiding eye contact with little emotion - good nor bad.

I walk up the stairs, counting each one, searching for some meaningless monotony to distract me from everything that's swirling down through my body, destined to blow out my ass at the worst possible time tonight. I was hoping for a downward escalator, but fuck me there's still only 17. I walk through the back of the restaurant with my head down as tension and sweat crawl over my body. One of the more enjoyably miserable waitresses sees me.

"What's wrong?" as far from farce as a terminally pissed waitress can be
"Everything" through a sigh that starts high and ends with the feeling behind it.

She almost laughs at first, maybe, probably thinking I'm joking, until she most likely realizes I'm not. She just kinda goes away, out of my site on my part, avoiding me for the rest of the night on hers. I don't blame her, or care. I don't like being around pissed off people. I only know how to make people laugh, but some times, most times, when people are like this they don't want to be cheered up. I can't talk about anything but women problems so less that, I just avoid it. I'm never like this for the greater majority. Maybe I have been. I know some of the nights I've been drinking a little more than needed I may have gotten a little nostalgic of that potential baby and its mother I so magically convinced myself I loved.

Wheew.

This is a good one tonight.

I'm standing in front of a table staring down at the plates in my hands, or the floor, or backwards into my head, or more likely the girl on the left's cleavage. Doesn't matter how depressed, I will love cleavage. I would rather her ass cheeks be bouncing up and down getting sprayed with oil out of a low pressured hose, but this is a family kinda spot at this hour.

I forget what any of the dishes are called so I just name something off the plate.

"Chicken?"

"That's me."

I throw both plates down and run away before the other realizes she got something with chicken too.

Usually would go get my mostly filled glass of water out of the server station, fill it up and go back in to flirt with whoever is willing to not leave right away.

I don't do that... and I'm actually thirsty this time too.

Back downstairs I'm not at the window, but back in the back hallway - unfinished and furnished with an upside down pickle bucket. The brick wall still sits 3 feet across from me, staring its normal stare. I don't try to move the brick with my mind, even though there's more energy running through me now than I can recall, more even than the time a girlfriend in college made me try coke for the first time - we banged for five hours without separating.

I get as close to sleep without actually doing any. I feel worse than when I sulked back here initially. My bell rings and I start drooling like a well-trained dog. I should be pissed but at least I have a resume builder in "well-trained". I scurry around the corner like a dog on a freshly waxed hardwood floor that's bound to crash into something expensive or someone's crotch. I lead head first around the corner to protect the fragile parts of my body and stop short of an old woman. She reminds me of my one great grandmother who I used to sneak up behind and scare. I used to be able to do that about every 4 minutes and she would never catch on, so I did it every 4 minutes until an adult realized what I was doing. The old lady almost shits herself. Doesn't matter if she did or not because she already smells like old people. She backs up and hesitates before saying "You should really slow down!" I don't like her tone so I respond "Probably!"

She's half way to the bathroom and most likely half dead as well when I hear someone laughing on the steps. It's a female laugh so I peak up the stairs. It's a quick look but I manage to catch a gorgeous figure in the low light. I pace around in a circle like the well trained mutt I am to get a second look.

"Well hey" stealing my line. It's her with the boyfriend. She walks down the stairs
"Well hey yourself" heart not even sinking, but completely disappearing.
"How have you been?" breaking stride - must not be an emergency.
"Could complain same shit meh." combining about 3 or 4 different answers into one.
"That so?" kinda laughing like 'oh you haven't changed'

"Meh.." nailing down an answer "How bout you?" thinking 'it's only been a month or so'.
"Good" high-pitched as in 'not good'
"That's good" lying to her face and kinda laughing like she did

I'm stuck now. If we have one more Q&A I'm going to be back and obsessed with her again. If I just snuff her, I may never see her again. When I say snuff I mean kill her because I really don't want to see her ever again. This is stupid. I hate feelings. I only have them when they aren't going to work out.

"I gotta pee bad" walking backwards turning around and kinda laughing again.
"Can I watch?" about the millionth time I've said that.
"Yeah, come on!"

She walks out of site and my head falls violently backwards like it would if I didn't consciously hold it up all the time.

There's food in the window.

I run it as fast as I can.

I hope she's shitting.

I get back and she's not here. I step casually around the corner to check as if she would run out the back employee exit to avoid me. She's back to wherever she came from.

Well...

Back to work.

I stare at the wall right next to the window to the kitchen for however long. The cooks can see me. I don't care much at all. The wall is dirty, but the kind of dirty you can only tell by standing three inches from it and staring for however long. Looks like invisible blood splatters running down from a recent massacre of some unsuspecting blond-big-titted virgin from a horror show.... or a group of redbull-vodka drinking early-twenty-somethings that got a little cheers happy and subconsciously decided to spill as much taurine as possible over as many things as they could see. I rest my head on the wall for a second before my depression subsides and I realize that that's gross. Rubbing my head like an itch I'm not supposed to scratch I hear a pitter-patter of a dream around the corner. The rubbing feels too good to stop before the steps trail around the corner and ask...

"What are you doing?"
"My head touched the wall and I realized how gross that is" still rubbing my head, half of my eyes open.

"Gross..."
"Gross? How 'bout the shit you just took in there huh?!" laughing before I get the whole sentence out
She laughs loud out of guilt "Hey! Girls do that too!"
"Not the ones I've met so far." disappointed I fell short of a creative comeback
"Well that's weird." just as disappointed as I am.
"So everything's good?" basically on my knees grasping at her heels trying to trip her so she can't leave yelling 'for the love of god don't go'
She does a huffy laugh and answers "Yup" and smiles seeing everything that's going on in my head right clearer than me now.
"Gotta get back to my friends. I think they are leaving"
"Alright... nice seeing you" tilting my head down so I have to look up to see her in an effort toward my seduction face of the last 20 years.
"Nice seeing you too..." with her hand kinda wiping my shoulder downward and turning to go up the stairs.

A life runs through my head - we were together and happy. We started out doing things that couples with no money do: walk in public, lay around naked, have sex on the stove that only has 1 functional burner and even that would putter out around 250 degrees. Both have a career we actually enjoy, not rich or anything but definitely not poor. Her head was on my lap in the living room of the arty-neat apartment on the couch and she says unprovoked "I'm happy". I smile and genuinely agree despite/in spite of the fact that we haven't done anything that anyone else would find close to entertaining or fun in a while. It's just the other that works for us. When she was pregnant she showed but was still the most beautiful thing I've ever seen. She never believed me when I told her because she always "felt fat". She was, but I never noticed. I would fall asleep with my face in her crotch. She always felt uncomfortable with this but I would tell her I just want to listen to the baby. It was half true. Our only kid, a daughter to my dismay at first, named something creative (by her suggestion and my absolute excitement), but not flower child stupid like 'rainbow', was the best, always laughing and never crying – although, she would by herself thinking about us as a family. I would walk in on her crying and be put in a fright, but she would just say "I'm happy" when I asked what was wrong. I wouldn't cry because I'm a man, but I would find it hard to choke out whatever I would respond with. Our unique daughter grew up to be successful in whatever she wanted to do. It didn't matter to me what, as long as it made her smile like her mother. We were parents at first, but more friends than anything when she was of a reasonable age. She moved away and we missed her terribly. Part of us was ready though. After 20-somethin years it was not bad having time to ourselves. We always make plans to see each other, but we understand that she has a life of her own with the husband and the baby on the way... she's preggers. Unfortunately for me she would die first. Partly expected on my part. I always thought that I had it too good for too long for something awful like that not to happen. I didn't leave the house for a while. Our daughter would call hoping I was better. I would say I'm fine and tell her to enjoy herself and I love her. I would then wander around my house picking up stuff and putting it right back while saying her name out loud. Suicide would be a frequent subject in my head even though I knew I was too much of a pussy to ever get close to attempting to kill myself. She would be laughing at me from wherever the heaven. Repeatedly I would ask her to kill me. She would just laugh from above and say "Get over yourself". This would make me smile. Finally it would be my time. Our daughter would be at bedside. Her husband would be there too. Before saying bye to her I would bring her husband in close, telling him "if you ever hurt her I will come back from wherever I am and kill you". He would laugh because I've told him this sorta thing multiple times since they met. He's a good guy. My daughter would hear this and be laugh-crying. I would just look at her and say "The hell's wrong with you? I'm old as fuck!" A peak of laughter would rise through the tears, not really helping. "Besides.." I would continue "I miss your mother" - as I stare at her butt bouncing away from me up the stairs.

I'm standing staring straight into the kitchen window listening to her walk up the last of the steps - 14,15,16. On the 17th there is a slight pause, an imagined one on my part, but it's something. Without looking up I yell up to her...

"You should give me a ring sometime."

She stops with her back foot on the 17th and slowly spins around, her shin-lengthed skirt-dress thing flows right behind.

"I don't have your number..." dress bouncing back to the middle
"...Call me.."
"Don't have your's either..." with a grin of *'you bitch!'* as she smiles, turns away and out of site.

My head's down and I'm still kinda smiling or something like, maybe even laughing softly for my own effect. It happens sometimes when I get in a situation that's a little emotional - I act like I would imagine how they would on TV. It makes me laugh when I realize what I'm doing. Realizing it, I laugh.
Her last smiling face.

This feels like a game.

Did I just lose?

Don't feel great.

That smiling bitch.

I lost.

Not because I didn't get her...

...but because I wanted to...

Well...

That sucks.

There's nothing coming up for a little bit so I walk around back to the regular kitchen door, the whole time kinda laughing about everything. I see one of the younger guys that smokes. Not wanting to hear some shit, I ask him for one instead of the others my age or older. He gives me one and I say something and head toward the back.

Wonder if it's raining.

Hope it's raining.

Probably not.

Walking down the long back hallway that smells like fishy shit, the cigarette is already hanging out of my mouth. Realizing I don't have a lighter - maybe it is raining - I turn around and yell back for one. The kid shuffles through his huge chef pants, pulls out a small yellow one and chucks it at me. Smoothly extending my hand to catch it, I drop it. "Thanks." yelling as I turn around almost prematurely lighting the thing out of a general frustration and impatience with everything.

Finally I'm out.

Not sure right away if it's raining or not. There's a few drops from the back deck above, but that could be from any drunk that spilled something there. It's shitty-looking out, strange for the area. There's a rumble somewhere. Looks like rain - doesn't mean there will be. Think I smell rain, but my sense of smell isn't my best one. Can't wait here all night. I light the cigarette and put the light back into my pocket like it were my own. I take an unnecessarily large puff and hold it in for some more effect. I manage to mumble 'what the fuck am I doing?' before exhaling. Toward the end of the exhale I think about how dramatic I'm being, laugh and immediately cough from the smoke going into some place uncomfortable from the laugh. I feel like throwing up. I fight the urge with some hair of the dog. It doesn't help, but I do feel shittier than before - was laughing too much considering the current events anyway. Good for me

Can I move on now?

Seems to be at an end.

A gust of wind streams underneath the deck. There's a strong garbage smell. Might've been the smell I mistook for rain earlier. It's hot out, but the moisture in the air hands out some chills. I hear or make believe there's some rain in the distance. I close my eyes and tilt my head back. Real or not the rain is getting closer

Why didn't she ask for my number that bitch!?

Should I have maybe asked for her number?

Jesus Fuck it happened again.

Don't think God likes that term much. It starts violently pouring...

I smile...
Drag the shit down to the filter... (flick the cigarette)
And stare off like I'm thinking about something.....

....or some shit I dunno....

www.ingramcontent.com/pod-product-compliance
Lightning Source LLC
Chambersburg PA
CBHW031354040426
42444CB00005B/284